NORMANDY 1
BATTLEFIELD RELICS

Régis GIARD

Histoire & Collections - Paris

Contents

For Adda and Louisa, my beloved children,
In memory of Louise, my dear grandmother

FOREWORD

As long as relics remain

With man not being immortal, the legacy of one's courage, commitment and sacrifice suffers the fate of being forgotten as time moves forward, however the survival of his battle equipment remains in place and not forgotten in 'Normandy 1944 Battlefield relics.'

From the pictures and history behind each article, the sting of battle and the glory of success is presented to preserve the legacy of those who liberated Europe and returned to its people that which have been taken away, their freedom.

Each article into itself tells a story of a soldier's day as he carried out his duty without question in support of the Allies.

General Patton was privileged to lead such men who were willing to sacrifice their all for the defeat of the Nazi Axis of Power. I am truly honoured to introduce you to this remembrance of those who gave us our today's.

George Patton Waters
Grandson, Gen. George S. Patton Jr.

The Field Boots of general George Smith Patton Jr.

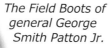

Close up of the medallion on the right heel.

For "Les" Brantingham

I was twenty years old, and Leslie was old enough to be my grandfather... a grandfather that I had just lost.

Leslie was a veteran of the 315th US Infantry Regiment, wounded on 4 July 1944 in front of 'Bloody Hill' in Normandy. He was, however, more than a veteran to me, as I had encountered a man and found a second family. Thanks to him, I visited the United States for the first time and my passion took on a whole new dimension. When he spoke in front of a gathering of veterans and families of his regiment on 2 September 2000 at Cincinnati, he also gave meaning to this passion. Seeing in my modest work the answers that some families were looking for, he encouraged me and in a certain way passed the baton on to another generation. I have never received a message as strong and straightforward as the one he gave me.

'Les' has gone, but his memory, via a few objects placed on my desk, will never leave me. My mission is not over....

Régis Giard

Good Conduct Medal and Combat Infantryman Badge belonging to Leslie R. Brantingham (315th Infantry, 79th US Infantry Division).

The longest days

The landing of 150,000 soldiers on five beaches on 6 June 1944 was not only a remarkable feat, but the operations in Normandy and Western France also forever transformed this part of the country. These battles, involving almost three million men, would decide in the space of a hundred days the fate of France and Europe.

Caen, a first day objective, would only fall after six weeks and four large-scale British offensives. To the West, the Americans took three weeks in capturing the port of Cherbourg and did not break out of the hedgerows until July. Gen. Patton and his armoured units then broke out into Brittany and towards the Loire river. The Mortain counter-attack, ordered by Hitler at the beginning of August, failed and forced the Germans into the trap of the Falaise Pocket. Those who managed to break out, squeezed by the Canadians in the north, the British in the west and the Americans in the south, were pursued and harried by the Allied air forces as far as the Seine.

The end of the 3rd Reich had begun...

Paris was liberated on 25 August 1944. By mid-September, the Allied forces in the north had linked up with those which had landed in Provence on 15 August, and the surrender of the fortresses of Le Havre and Brest brought an end to the opening of a second front that the Soviet allies had been awaiting for so long.

By the autumn, Normandy was part of the rear-echelon areas which supported the advance towards Germany. Airfields and field hospitals were set up alongside prisoner of war camps and cemeteries, scattered from the blood-drenched sands of Omaha Beach and beyond to the ruins of Saint-Lô, the burnt wheat fields of Hill 112 and the killing fields of the 'corridor of death' in the Falaise Pocket.

Of relics and men

Just as the northern and eastern regions of France rose from the ashes after the Great War, Normandy, after having been the scene of one of the largest battles of the Second World War, would slowly rebuild itself and become a land of Remembrance.

The war was forgotten somewhat but, after the difficult period of reconstruction, men – and a few women – would begin to find and conserve relics that bore witness to the fighting.

This trend grew steadily under the impulse of young third-generation Normans, but the historical value of these objects only became apparent later. Indeed, it is only now, with the fading away of those who had witnessed the fighting, that these modest remains can now be construed in a new light and help understand larger events.

This publication is not just about presenting these historical objects, but also what they lived through, as well as allowing their enthusiastic safe keepers to show them to a wider audience. It is also a wonderful opportunity to remember all the men who took part in the Battle of Normandy seventy years ago.

Régis Giard

LET'S GO!

Before Eisenhower's final "Let's go!" heralding one of the greatest combined operations of all time, the Allies would have to succeed in uniting all of their efforts in this "great crusade for a free world."

Four years after the invasion of Poland by the armies of the Reich, and with war gone global, the objective consisted of establishing a bridgehead in north-west France, allowing for a direct advance on Berlin. Roosevelt had made this his doctrine and foresaw it as early as 1942, but Churchill was more for a strategy of the gradual wearing down of Axis forces. Although the operation, named 'Overlord,' had been in the planning phase since the beginning of 1943, it was Stalin who finally forced the issue during the Tehran conference in November.

If Great Britain, the only free bastion capable of holding a gigantic armada, soon became the obvious choice as a springboard for such an operation, the Allied staffs soon chose Normandy as the best compromise for an operation of this scale.

Further away from Great Britain, but also less defended than the Pas-de-Calais, the relatively low coastline between the mouths of the Orne and the Vire rivers remained within an acceptable operational range as far as logistics and air support were concerned.

As well as the amazing achievement of setting up an organisation capable of coordinating the actions of the French Underground, Allied paratroopers and assault troops, naval and air support, or the construction of artificial ports and an underwater pipeline, another challenge arose, that of obtaining, despite the magnitude of the task, total surprise.

During the night of 5 June 1944, a thousand planes dropped paratroopers over Brittany, the mouth of the river Orne and in the Cotentin, but the Germans still believed this was another raid. By continuing to bomb objectives in the Pas-de-Calais or by billeting a fictitious army group in Kent, the Allies kept up the illusion of a main offensive in the Pas-de-Calais or Norway, the potential objectives favoured by the German high command.

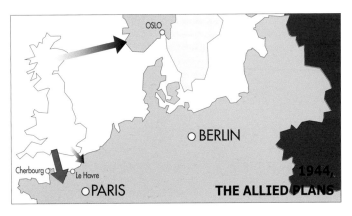

"THE DICE ARE ROLLED..."

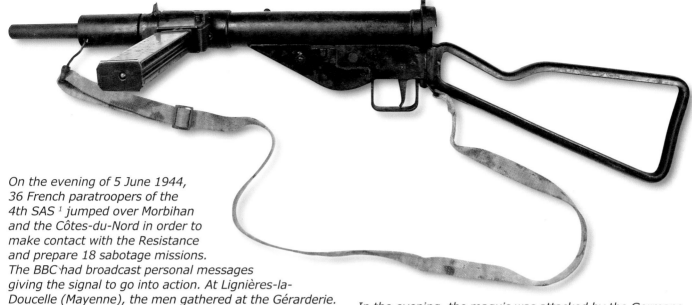

On the evening of 5 June 1944, 36 French paratroopers of the 4th SAS [1] jumped over Morbihan and the Côtes-du-Nord in order to make contact with the Resistance and prepare 18 sabotage missions. The BBC had broadcast personal messages giving the signal to go into action. At Lignières-la-Doucelle (Mayenne), the men gathered at the Gérarderie. The 'Tortoise' plan was set in motion against German convoys moving towards Normandy.

This British Sten Mk II machine carbine was used by 19 year old Paul Lasnier, a member of the Lignères maquis from the Ille-et-Vilaine department. Wounded on the morning of 13 June, he was captured in the afternoon.

In the evening, the maquis was attacked by the Germans and Paul Lasnier was executed along with eight of his comrades.

1. The 4th Regiment of the Special Air Service in the British order of battle, and the '2e régiment de chasseurs parachutistes' in that of Free France.

WACHT AM KANAL

Given the impossibility of buttressing the entire 5,000 km coast from Holland to Spain with concrete defences, the Germans designed a defensive system that would block the invader with obstacles laid out along the entire depth of the beach. On the coast, strongpoints (Widerstandnester-Wn) were bolstered by barbed wire and minefields. Wn61, to the east of Omaha Beach, comprised of a 88 mm gun in a casemate, a dug-in 50 mm gun, a tank turret, two machine-gun nests and a flame thrower.

This concrete batch sample, dated 8 May 1944 and found on Wn61, highlights perfectly the situation of the Atlantikwall at the time of the invasion. Although overall more than a third of the defences were completed, in Normandy it is estimated that this was the case for only half.

"HAM AND JAM"

This was the coded message sent by Major John Howard, CO of D Company/2 Oxfordshire and Buckinghamshire Light Infantry to announce the success of the first elements of the 6th Airborne Division during the night of 6 June 1944. Shortly after midnight, the 180 men under his command landed in six gliders and took the bridges at Bénouville (later known as 'Pegasus Bridge') and Ranville. Four thousand British paratroopers arrived after and, despite problems encountered in assembling, managed to take their objectives. The 5th Parachute Brigade relieved Howard's men and set up forward positions to the east of the two bridges over the Orne and the Caen canal.

The 3rd Parachute Brigade destroyed five bridges over the Dives whilst the 9th Parachute Battalion landed near the Merville battery, knocking out the heavy guns that posed a threat to Sword Beach.

This British paratrooper's helmet, found near the Seine, also highlights the long campaign which awaited the 6th Airborne Division after 6 June. They only returned to Britain in September, after defending the Orne bridgehead for three months and accompanying the advance to the Seine.

BOSTON AND ALBANY

During the night of 5-6 June, 13,000 American paratroopers of the 82nd and 101st Airborne Divisions were dropped behind Utah Beach. In the initial plan, the paras would drop between Barneville-sur-Mer and Carentan, securing the line of marshes whilst the force landed at Utah would drive for Cherbourg. However, a few days before the assault, the presence of the 91. Luftlande-Division in the midst of this area forced a change. Three regiments of the 82nd would drop just to the west of Sainte-Mère-Eglise (mission 'Boston'). Behind Utah Beach, the men of the 101st Airborne had been tasked with protecting the landing force from the German reaction and taking control of the bridges and main crossroads that would help the infantry exit the beach areas ('Albany').

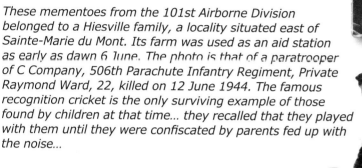

These mementoes from the 101st Airborne Division belonged to a Hiesville family, a locality situated east of Sainte-Marie du Mont. Its farm was used as an aid station as early as dawn 6 June. The photo is that of a paratrooper of C Company, 506th Parachute Infantry Regiment, Private Raymond Ward, 22, killed on 12 June 1944. The famous recognition cricket is the only surviving example of those found by children at that time... they recalled that they played with them until they were confiscated by parents fed up with the noise...

THE DEATH OF GENERAL FALLEY

On the evening of 5 June, Generalleutnant Wilhelm Falley, commanding the 91. Luftlande-Division which had arrived in Normandy in May 1944, was making his way to Rennes in order to take part in a Kriegspiel, a table-top war game whose theme was an invasion of Normandy by airborne forces... However, fearful of the planes flying overhead, Falley decided to turn-around and return to his headquarters at the château de Bernaville near Picauville. Less than a kilometre from his HQ, he fell into an ambush set up by a dozen American paratroopers at the Minoterie farm. Hearing the approaching car, the paras hid on either side of the road. Lieutenant Brannen (above, right) tried to stop the car, but the driver accelerated and the Americans opened fire all at the same time. The driver lost control and the Horch crashed into the farm (see the 8 June aerial photo, above, centre). Falley was killed.

Major Joachim Bartuzat, his aide de camp, was apparently shot whilst attempting to pick up his pistol. The injured driver was taken prisoner. The first German general had just died in Normandy.

This wheel-hub cover from Falley's staff car was found a few years later in a ditch at the site of the ambush.

THE PRICE OF LIBERTY

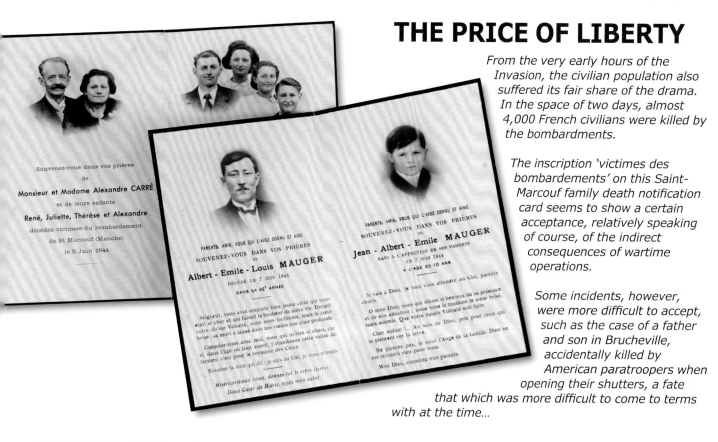

From the very early hours of the Invasion, the civilian population also suffered its fair share of the drama. In the space of two days, almost 4,000 French civilians were killed by the bombardments.

The inscription 'victimes des bombardements' on this Saint-Marcouf family death notification card seems to show a certain acceptance, relatively speaking of course, of the indirect consequences of wartime operations.

Some incidents, however, were more difficult to accept, such as the case of a father and son in Brucheville, accidentally killed by American paratroopers when opening their shutters, a fate that which was more difficult to come to terms with at the time...

SILENT WINGS

At dawn on 6 June 1944, paratroopers received reinforcements brought in by gliders. In the British sector, no less than 300 Horsa and 30 large Hamilcar gliders landed without major mishap. In the American sector, the landing of almost 300 CG-4 Waco gliders and a little more than 200 Horsas was haphazard. The approach to the main landing zone, partially occupied by the Germans, made it necessary to land in fields which were too short or cluttered with obstacles.

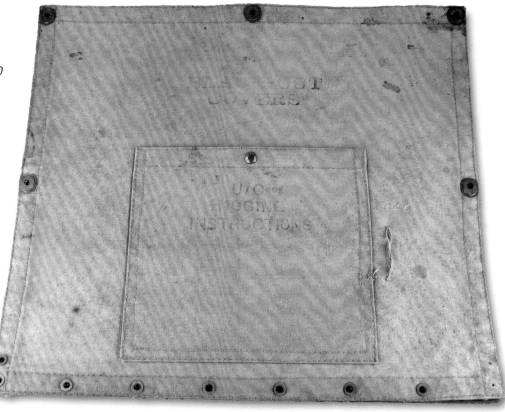

This black-out curtain from a Horsa glider was found amongst wreckage near Blosville in the American sector.

D-DAY

The invasion began at dawn on 6 June 1944. The young American nation was coming to the rescue of the Old Continent.

Contrary to 1917, in 1944 the United States had a strategy and an army which now formed the largest Allied contingent. It had at its disposal previously unheard of means that had been supplied by the 'Arsenal of Democracy' set up by Roosevelt. However, although the Supreme Commander of the expeditionary forces was the American General Dwight D. Eisenhower, the three main commands were entrusted to the British Ramsay, Leigh-Mallory and Montgomery, respectively for the navy, air forces and ground forces.

Thus, according to the plan laid down by Operation 'Neptune,' the landings would be undertaken almost simultaneously by five infantry divisions along 80 kilometres of coastline. Two American divisions would land at Utah and Omaha beaches between Sainte-Marie du Mont and Colleville-sur-Mer. Between them, the Rangers would capture the battery at Pointe du Hoc. A Canadian division and two British divisions, as well as a few Frenchmen, would land at Gold, Juno and Sword beaches between Port en Bessin and Ouistreham. The initial assault would comprise of approximately 150,000 men and 20,000 vehicles, transported by a fleet of 5,000 vessels and supported by 10,000 fighter and bomber aircraft dropping 5,000 tonnes of bombs on the German defences.

This demonstration of power underlines the decisive character of the operation and the determination of the Allies not to repeat past mistakes. The intelligence services came to the conclusion that twenty German divisions, eight of which were armoured, would be able to counter-attack within three days, the bridgehead therefore had to be rapidly expanded in order to avoid becoming bogged down as had been the case in Italy.

By the evening of the 'Longest day,' Allied losses were a little more than 10,000 men and all objectives had not been achieved, but overall the landings were a success, the five beaches had been secured. On 7 June, two German armoured divisions failed in their attempt to push the British back to the sea. The following day, Bayeux fell and on the 14th, the bridgehead was consolidated. Although the Germans were beginning to realise that this was the invasion, on 15 June 1944, a raid involving 300 British bombers on Boulogne sur Mer continued to divert their attention to the Pas-de-Calais.

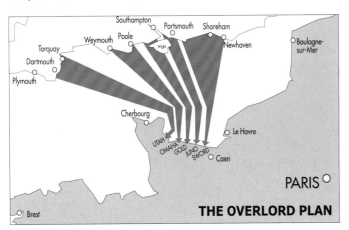

THE OVERLORD PLAN

POINTE DU HOC

The Pointe du Hoc is a piece of land which juts out at the top of thirty-metre high cliffs. It had a battery comprising of six 155 mm guns, positioned between Omaha and Utah beaches. A force of 225 men of the 2nd Ranger Battalion was tasked with climbing the cliffs and destroying the guns. The objective, already heavily bombed since the spring, was hit a final time by naval guns just before the assault.

This naval shell splinter (360 mm) was found at Pointe du Hoc in the 1970s, before the area was placed under the protection of, and partially ceded to, the United States. Between 05.50 and 06.25 on 6 June, the USS Texas fired 255 shells of this calibre onto the Pointe du Hoc, the battleship's heaviest concentration of the entire war.

LA MADELEINE, A.K.A. UTAH BEACH

Although the aerial bombardment of the beach at Utah was inaccurate, the naval shelling was not and destroyed the majority of the German defences. As the plan had stipulated, twelve amphibious Sherman tanks and sixteen other armoured vehicles attacked at 06.30 hrs. Having arrived with the first wave of 600 men of the 8th Infantry (4th US Infantry Division), General Theodore Roosevelt realised that the landing had taken place two kilometres from where it should have. He took the decision for the following units to arrive at the same spot. Thus, the beach of La Madeleine, at Sainte-Marie-du-Mont, became Utah Beach. On 6 June at dusk, 20,000 men had set foot there, for losses of less than 200.

This water breaker held drinking water on the small landing craft. 4,000 such vessels were used for the D-Day operations.

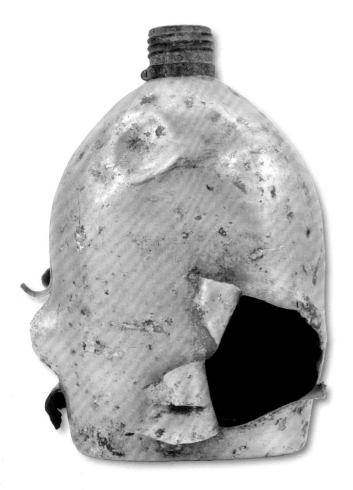

Pfc. Lawyer

NO FURTHER DETAILS...

At Omaha too, the first wave was disorganised by the strong currents. Almost all of the amphibious tanks sank and the naval shelling had not destroyed the defences. Having landed from 07.40 hrs onwards, the first half-tracks of the Anti-tank Company, 16th Infantry (1st US Infantry Division) were pinned down on the beach. With most of their officers killed or wounded, the mixed-up and leaderless units took shelter behind a bank of shingle. Pushed forward by the rising tide, on their own initiative, at around 08.00 hrs, small groups began to tackle the strongpoints. These actions opened breaches in the defences and, by the evening of 6 June, 'Bloody Omaha' was captured, despite losses of 4,000 out of the 34,000 men who were landed there.

This water bottle, found at Omaha Beach in the 1980s, belonged to Pfc Allan Bennett Lawyer (Anti-tank company, 16th Infantry), who was posted as missing on 6 June 1944. Following the confirmation of his death, the local newspaper stated that this 25-year old soldier, one of five sons serving in the army, had taken part in the North African, Sicilian and Italian campaigns. The article ends stating that no details had been forwarded to the family.

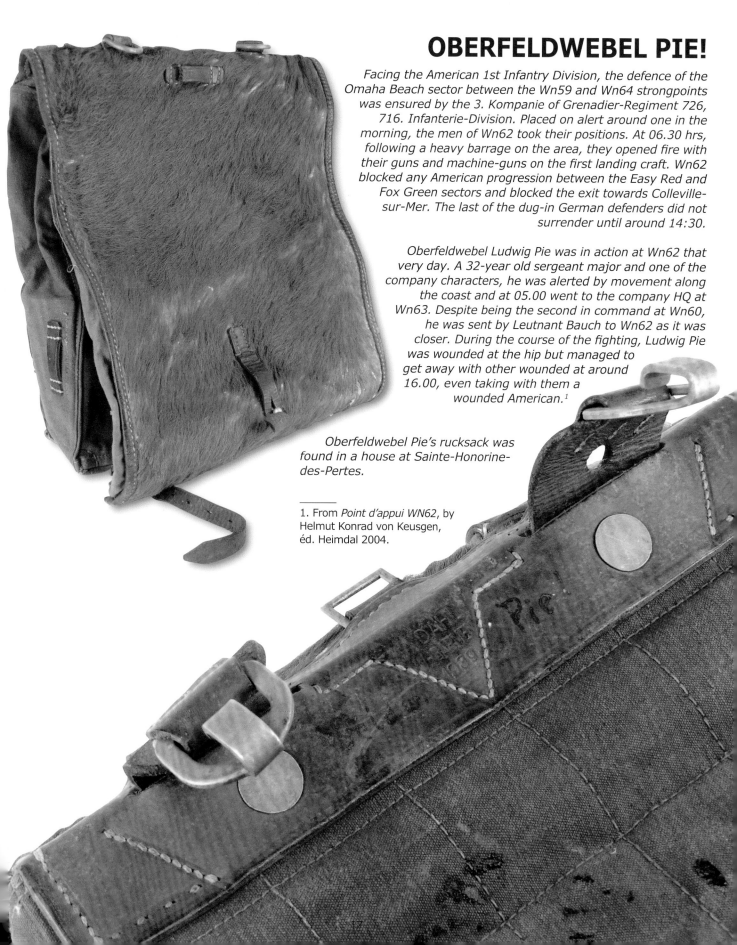

OBERFELDWEBEL PIE!

Facing the American 1st Infantry Division, the defence of the Omaha Beach sector between the Wn59 and Wn64 strongpoints was ensured by the 3. Kompanie of Grenadier-Regiment 726, 716. Infanterie-Division. Placed on alert around one in the morning, the men of Wn62 took their positions. At 06.30 hrs, following a heavy barrage on the area, they opened fire with their guns and machine-guns on the first landing craft. Wn62 blocked any American progression between the Easy Red and Fox Green sectors and blocked the exit towards Colleville-sur-Mer. The last of the dug-in German defenders did not surrender until around 14:30.

Oberfeldwebel Ludwig Pie was in action at Wn62 that very day. A 32-year old sergeant major and one of the company characters, he was alerted by movement along the coast and at 05.00 went to the company HQ at Wn63. Despite being the second in command at Wn60, he was sent by Leutnant Bauch to Wn62 as it was closer. During the course of the fighting, Ludwig Pie was wounded at the hip but managed to get away with other wounded at around 16.00, even taking with them a wounded American.[1]

Oberfeldwebel Pie's rucksack was found in a house at Sainte-Honorine-des-Pertes.

1. From *Point d'appui WN62*, by Helmut Konrad von Keusgen, éd. Heimdal 2004.

GOLD, JUNO AND SWORD

On 6 June, the British 50th (Northumbrian) Infantry Division succeeded in getting off Gold Beach and advancing ten kilometres inland towards Bayeux. Despite a more difficult landing, the 3rd Canadian Infantry Division, at Juno Beach, moved close to its objective at Carpiquet near Caen. The British 3rd Infantry Division (Sword Beach), made a successful link-up with the 6th Airborne via the bridge at Bénouville, but remained cut-off from the Canadians due to the counter-attack led by the 21. Panzer-Division. Although around a thousand British and a thousand Canadians were killed on the first day, more than 50,000 British had landed and for the Canadians this figure was 20,000. Caen, the ambitious D-Day objective, had not been taken yet.

This British Mark II helmet, found at Hermanville-sur-Mer, bears the white stripe specific to the Beach Groups. The two bars at the front and rear designate a signals unit. At Hermanville, on Sword Beach, the signals of No 5 and No 6 Beach Groups were ensured by the 101st Beach Sub-Area Signal Section.

ONE HUNDRED AND SEVENTY-SEVEN

Volunteering in 1940 with the Free French Navy (Forces Navales Françaises Libres- FNFL), enseigne de vaisseau de 2e classe Jean Mazéas was assigned service No 5745FN40. Having joined the 1er Bataillon de Fusiliers Marins led by capitaine de corvette Philippe Kieffer, he landed on 6 June 1944 at Ouistreham with Troop 1 of No 4 Commando. The 177 French volunteers[1] of the Commando Kieffer captured the Riva-Bella and the casino bunker. Jean Mazéas was seriously wounded in the arm and evacuated on 6 June. 33 others were wounded and ten killed.

Jean Mazéas' cap was made in 1943 by Lillywhites of London. It bears the stripes of a Capitaine de corvette, his last rank before returning to civilian life in February 1946.

1. The 177 were in fact 171 French, four Luxemburgers, a Pole and a Canadian.

THE BEGINNING OF THE END

Facing the 4th US Infantry Division at Utah were elements of the German 709. Infanterie-Division, whereas units of the 352. Infanterie-Division opposed the American 29th Infantry Division at Omaha Beach. From Colleville-sur-Mer up to the river Orne, the entire 716. Infanterie-Division faced the American 1st Infantry Division as well as the British 50th, Canadian 3rd and British 3rd Infantry Divisions.

The Allied propaganda services made the most of the fate suffered by the 716th, a third of which comprised of Osttruppen[1], in order to encourage other units in Normandy to cease fighting. This tract announcing "The end of a division" is a so-called detailed report from the survivors, now 'safe' in Britain after having been abandoned by "their own side, without infantry reinforcements, tanks or planes...

1. The Osttruppen were former Soviet prisoners of war enrolled into the German army. In the 716th division, they were mostly Russians and Ukrainians.

DAS ENDE EINER DIVISION

Überlebende der 716. I.D. (Kreml-Division) sind jetzt in Sicherheit in England. Ihre Berichte sind **EINE WARNUNG FÜR ALLE TRUPPEN AM ATLANTIKWALL — DIE AUF ENTSATZ WARTEN.**

Hier ist einer der Berichte :

„Am Dienstag war der erste Angriff auf unseren Abschnitt zwischen Arromanches und Ouistreham. Da kriegten wir gleich den Befehl : Aushalten — Verstärkung im Anmarsch !

Am Donnerstag waren wir praktisch schon überrannt und eingekesselt. Rückwärts war der Feind mit kanadischen Fallschirmjägern. Vorne lag der Feind mit Schlachtschiffen und zerhackte uns die Stellung. Und über uns da hing der Feind mit einer dicken Fliegerdecke und jagte uns mit Flächenwürfen die letzten Minenfelder hoch.

Kein deutscher Jäger zu sehen. Keine Verbindung mehr mit rechts und links — alles was wir wussten war : der Anglo-Amerikaner landet dauernd Truppen und schweres Material auf beiden Seiten.

Und von Verstärkung keine Rede. Nur wieder der Befehl vom Kommandeur kam durch : Aushalten bis zum letzten Schuss !

Da lagen wir so gut wie nackt in unseren ausgeschlitzten Bunkern und sollten mit unseren Maschinenpistolen und

ZG. II

THE BRIDGE...

On 6 June, La Fière and Chef-du-Pont were, along with Sainte-Mère-Eglise, the main objectives of the US 82nd Airborne Division. The most important phase of the mission entailed the rapid capture of Cherbourg. The two bridges over the Merderet were the only areas which allowed the Americans to advance towards the west. From dawn onwards, a group of men from the 507th Parachute Infantry Regiment (PIR) gathered west of La Fière. As this group was not strong enough, they had to wait for the attack of other paratroopers arriving from the east in order to advance and successfully link up near Cauquigny. Just when the sector seemed secure, heavy German artillery opened up before an attack by grenadiers

and light tanks dispersed the bulk of the paratroopers. The La Fière causeway was rapidly lost but the American forces on each side of the marshes held their ground. At around 17.00 hrs, the Germans returned in force accompanied by three tanks to the bridge at La Fière. However, they were stopped by a handful of 505 PIR paratroopers.

This manufacturer's plate was found on the bed of the Merderet in 2013 and comes from one of the two [1] Renault R35 tanks of Panzer Ersatz-und-Ausbildungsabteilung 100 destroyed on 6 June on the La Fière causeway.

_____

1. These were French tanks captured in 1940, the third tank destroyed was a Hotchkiss H39.

... AT LA FIÈRE

Near the manor house at La Fière, two bazooka teams, as well as two machine-guns, were ready to spring an ambush from the ditches on each side of the road. A 57 mm anti-tank gun was set up further up the road. When the first German tank halted, the machine-gunners killed the tank commander in his turret. The bazookas opened fire but the tank fired back. Marcus Heim, the loader and Peterson the bazooka man, continued firing until a young paratrooper stopped the tank by dropping a grenade into the turret. Heim and Peterson fired at the second tank. Having run out of projectiles, Heim crossed the road to fetch the rockets left by another team. Once the weapon was reloaded, they stopped the last tank and the Germans withdrew. The attacks continued and on the evening of 7 June, elements of the 325th Glider Infantry Regiment (GIR) relieved the 505th. The causeway was finally cleared after the last fighting on 9 June.

This musette bag belonged to Marcus Heim. For their actions at La Fière, Heim, Peterson, Bolderson and Pryne (bazooka) were decorated with the Distinguished Service Cross (the second highest award for bravery in action). Marcus Heim received his DSC at the beginning of July from the hands of General Bradley at Brocqueboeuf manor, east of La Haye-du-Puits

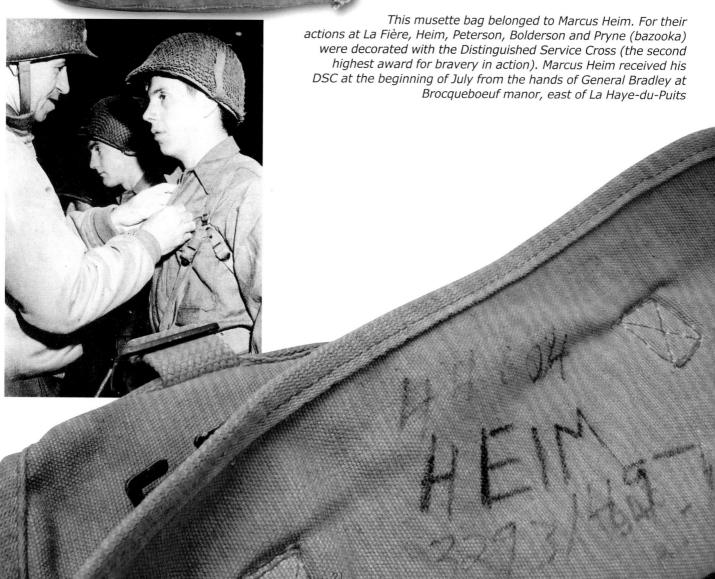

Objective Cherbourg

A deep water port for unloading men, weapons, food, ammunition, fuel..., this was the priority objective once the beaches had been linked up.

The raid on Dieppe on 19 August 1942 had proved the impossibility of a frontal attack against a harbour, and the difficulty of the Salerno landings towards Naples in 1943 showed that it was necessary to act quickly until a port could be captured.

The landings at Utah aimed at seizing Cherbourg in short order, and the schedule placed the port and the Querqueville petrol terminal in the hands of the Allies only within a fortnight. The solution came from British strategists. Eight days after the landings, their artificial ports were operational off the coast at Saint-Laurent sur Mer and Arromanches.

The task which remained for the Americans was cutting off the Cotentin peninsula, blocking the movement of German reinforcements from the south and then leading the assault on 'Festung' (fortress) Cherbourg. Struggling in front of Caen, the Anglo-Canadian forces, unable to open the road towards the Seine and Paris, pinned down the Panzer divisions.

On 17 June, the Americans cut off the base of the peninsula by reaching Barneville sur Mer, but their advance through the hedgerow countryside had been arduous. The pivoting movement northwards was not carried out straight away. This attack was only launched on 19 June, whereas the Channel was being hit by a storm which would batter the artificial harbours and complicate matters for the logistical support units.

However, the Germans did not make the most of this. By refusing to undertake a strategic withdrawal to the Seine, behind which the bulk of the reserves were stationed, Hitler lost the opportunity to save the 50,000 men in the Cotentin.

Despite the fact that General von Schlieben and Rear-admiral Hennecke, commanding respectively Cherbourg and the Kriegsmarine in Normandy, refused the ultimatum issued by General Lawton Collins (US VII Corps) on the 22nd, they capitulated on 26 June in the face of three infantry divisions and their impressive air and naval support. But they only yielded a landscape of ruins, for the entire port infrastructure had been systematically destroyed. The first freight ship would not be able to moor until a month later...

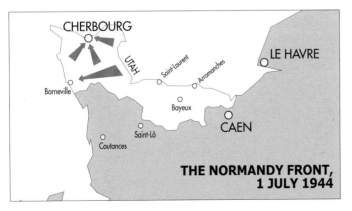

THE NORMANDY FRONT, 1 JULY 1944

SAINT-SAUVEUR LE VICOMTE

The 90th US Infantry Division, tasked with the main effort of isolating the Cotentin peninsula, had received the order to take Saint-Sauveur-le-Vicomte. However, it encountered difficulties on 14 June and the 82nd Airborne attacked in support along the road from Pont-l'Abbé to Saint-Sauveur, whilst at the same time the 9th Infantry Division pushed further north. On 15 June, the 325th GIR was at Rauville-la-Place, less than a kilometre from Saint-Sauveur. Supported by tanks, elements of the 82nd Division were on the east bank of the Douve by midday on 16 June. As for the Germans, they set up two 'Kampfgruppe' for the defence of Cherbourg and to ensure an escape route along the west coast. They pulled out of Saint-Sauveur and the American paratroopers entered the town. On 18 June, the 9th Division was at Barneville-sur-Mer and the Cotentin was definitively cut in two.

This steel helmet was found at Saint-Sauveur-le-Vicomte. It belonged to a member of the Communications Platoon, HQ Company/505th Parachute Infantry Regiment (82nd Airborne Division).

"KENNY" MCDONALD,

Having landed at Utah Beach on 14 June 1944, the 79th US Infantry Division began advancing on Cherbourg on the 19th, around Valognes by the west in order to take up positions on the main road to the north. At five in the morning, the attack began under heavy rain. Around 14.00 hrs, the 313th Infantry Regiment made the main effort and captured the Bois de la Brique. The progression of the 315th was slower. A battalion became pinned-down less than two kilometres after leaving Urville. In the afternoon, the 2nd battalion of Pfc Kenneth J. McDonald was counter-attacked in the Yvetot-Bocage sector. The battle lasted for four hours. G Company was ordered to mop-up the hamlet of Grand Saint-Lin, on the western edge of Valognes. It was at this exact place that McDonald was seriously wounded by a shell splinter whilst attempting to cross the Valognes – Bricquebec road.

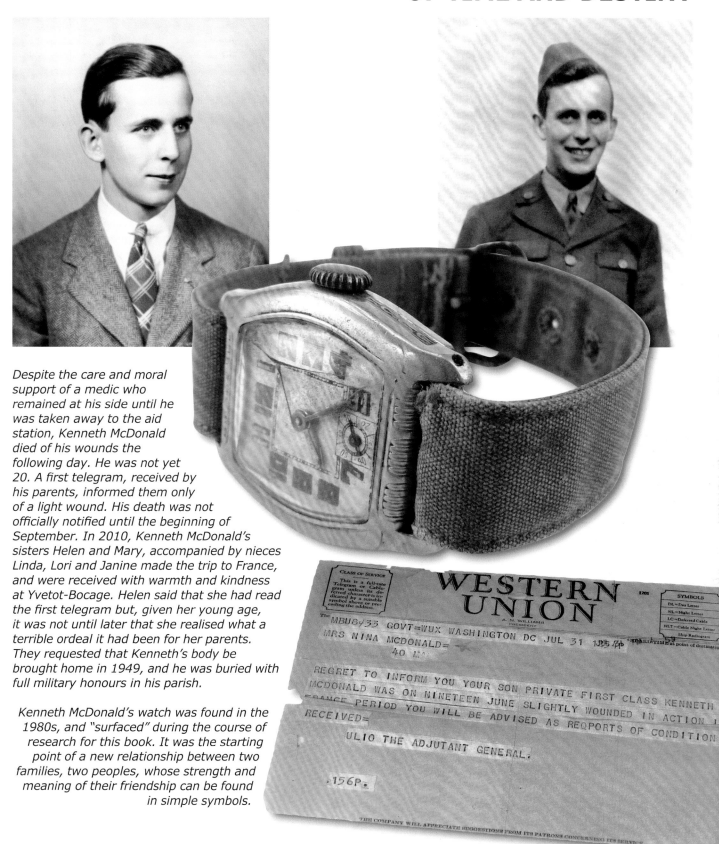

Despite the care and moral support of a medic who remained at his side until he was taken away to the aid station, Kenneth McDonald died of his wounds the following day. He was not yet 20. A first telegram, received by his parents, informed them only of a light wound. His death was not officially notified until the beginning of September. In 2010, Kenneth McDonald's sisters Helen and Mary, accompanied by nieces Linda, Lori and Janine made the trip to France, and were received with warmth and kindness at Yvetot-Bocage. Helen said that she had read the first telegram but, given her young age, it was not until later that she realised what a terrible ordeal it had been for her parents. They requested that Kenneth's body be brought home in 1949, and he was buried with full military honours in his parish.

Kenneth McDonald's watch was found in the 1980s, and "surfaced" during the course of research for this book. It was the starting point of a new relationship between two families, two peoples, whose strength and meaning of their friendship can be found in simple symbols.

WESTERN UNION

SYMBOLS
DL=Day Letter
NL=Night Letter
LC=Deferred Cable
NLT=Cable Night Letter
Ship Radiogram

MBU8433 GOVT=WUX WASHINGTON DC JUL 31 1945

MRS NINA MCDONALD=
40 M

REGRET TO INFORM YOU YOUR SON PRIVATE FIRST CLASS KENNETH MCDONALD WAS ON NINETEEN JUNE SLIGHTLY WOUNDED IN ACTION I FRANCE PERIOD YOU WILL BE ADVISED AS REQPORTS OF CONDITION RECEIVED=

ULIO THE ADJUTANT GENERAL.

.156P.

THE DUCK POND

On 20 June, the Americans had reached the main defensive line at Cherbourg. General von Schlieben and the Cotentin defenders had fallen back into the fortress upon Hitler's orders, which stipulated that they were to fight to the last man. On 21 June, Gen. Collins sent an ultimatum demanding their surrender and on the 22nd, as this had remained unanswered, he launched the 9th, 79th and 4th US Infantry Divisions. The German defence in depth was anchored on large fortifications and the 79th had to tackle those at Chèvres (Tollevast) and the Mare à Canards (the 'duck pond,' near La Glacerie) before reaching the fort du Roule overlooking Cherbourg. However, air support was ineffective on the bunkers and, despite the heavy bombardments of the 22nd and those by fighter-bombers the next day, the 314th Infantry Regiment had to repeat its attacks before taking the two main positions of La Mare à Canards. On the evening of the 25th, the 79th had reached Fort du Roule, the 9th was at Equeurdreville and Octeville and the 4th had entered the port via Tourlaville. The end of 'Festung Cherbourg' was in sight.

This French fireman's helmet from the La Glacerie fire brigade was taken home by a now deceased American veteran. It returned from California to France in 2012.

MAJOR FRIEDRICH KÜPPERS

On 26 June, a helmeted General von Schlieben left his underground headquarters at Octeville and accepted the demand to surrender. But, on the 27th, Panzerwerk Osteck, a group of thirty blockhaus in the Carneville plains was still holding out. Major Küppers, commander of the 'Montebourg' battery, laid his guns and pushed back no less than four tank attacks. By the evening, the 22nd Infantry of the 4th US Infantry Division found a way through the thin minefield. Surrounded on the morning of the 28th, Küppers accepted to enter into talks. General Barton (the divisional commander) personally showed his plan of attack should negotiations fail, and the major could see that there was no point in fighting on. [1]

This army trunk belonging to Major Friedrich Küppers was found at Gonneville, near the Osteck battery.

_____
1. From *Invasion! they are coming,* Paul Carell, 1963.

PLUTO

15,000 tonnes of fuel was the estimated daily requirement on D+41 (15 July). Although the port of Cherbourg had been captured, the hopes placed in its logistical value were dashed. The harbour was in ruins and sabotaged to such an extent that Admiral Hennecke, the man tasked with its destruction, was awarded the Knight's Cross of the Iron Cross. Although the American engineers deployed colossal efforts, the PLUTO (Pipe-Line Under The Ocean) linking the Isle of Wight with the Querqueville terminal was only operational from August onwards. In the meantime, the temporary terminals of Port-en-Bessin and Saint-Honorine-des-Pertes continued supplying the main fuel dump at Mont-Cauvin.

This pipe-line collar is a reminder of the Mont-Cauvin installations at Etréham.

HEDGEROW HELL

On 26 June, Montgomery regained the initiative towards the Odon river, but once more, the SS armoured divisions blocked the way to Caen.

By 1 July 1944, more than 20,000 GI's had been lost, but the main effort still fell to the US Army.

When planning the breakout of four American corps towards Coutances, then Brittany, however, it seems it had underestimated the terrain, the German forces and their tactics. Also, the rain hindered tactical air support and movement of mechanised transport.

The breakout towards the south had to cross terrain which the French military engineer Vauban had deemed in 1686 almost "unsuitable for carts and cavalry." The hills and sunken narrow roads, the meadows surrounded by thick hedgerows and wide ditches, rivers and boggy marshes, were natural elements used to perfection by the German defenders.

Hitler was aiming to contain the enemy and gain time in order to bring into play his new weapons (rockets and jet planes). Thus, the German high command had built up a mobile reserve of panzers, Waffen-SS and paratroopers in order to intervene rapidly against any breakthrough in the main line of defence.

Towards La Haye-du-Puits, Sainteny and Saint-Lô, the Americans only launched frontal attacks mainly carried out by infantry. But the hedgerows cut off the point elements in the midst of small meadows where German machine-guns and mortars cut them down.

At Saint-Jean-de-Daye, the Americans lost the opportunity to break through. Confusing speed and haste, they created a terrible traffic jam in the tiny bridgehead beneath the canal of Vire and Taute.

Finding themselves in front of Lessay and Périers, but halted in front of Saint-Lô for three weeks, the GIs thought that the fighting in the hedgerows would last for months. Coutances seemed as far off as Berlin at this time! 40,000 more men had been lost and moral was at a low ebb, the time had come to change tactics.

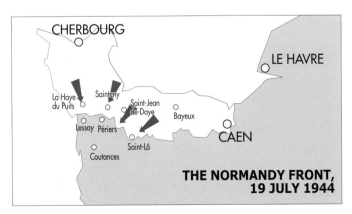

THE NORMANDY FRONT, 19 JULY 1944

LEON W. VASSAR

On 3 July, the 82nd Airborne Division was tasked with its final mission in Normandy. It had to establish a solid jumping off point for the 'green' men of the 8th Infantry

Division. Following a three-day battle, the paratroopers captured a front some seven kilometres in depth and took their objectives to the north and east of La Haye-du-Puits. Mont Etenclin, the hill of Sainte-Catherine and the high ground at Brocquebœuf and la Poterie were the sites of their last exploits in Normandy. On 13 July 1944, the few survivors of the division left for England from Utah Beach.

The spoon bearing the name and service number of Leon W. Vassar, a paratrooper with the 505th PIR and a machine-gunner in the first platoon of H Company, was found in the Poterie sector at Lithaire. In the photo taken in England at Camp Quorn (where the company was stationed from mid-February to the end of May 1944), we can see (as was common practice) the spoon placed in the breast pocket of Private Vassar.

CONCENTRATION 55 AT 'GLAUGNY'

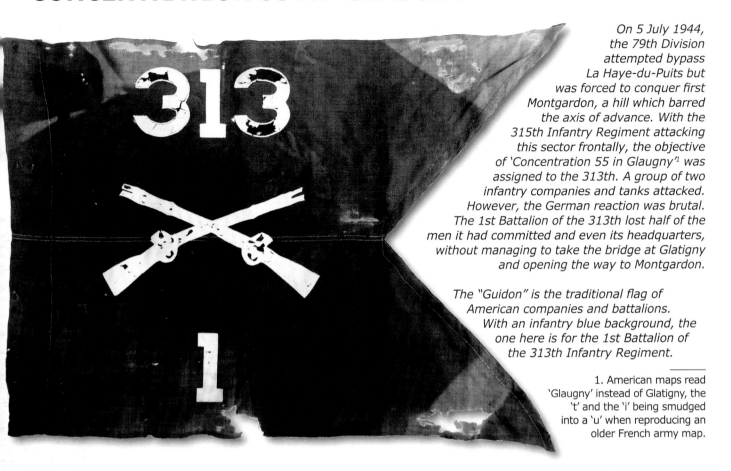

On 5 July 1944, the 79th Division attempted bypass La Haye-du-Puits but was forced to conquer first Montgardon, a hill which barred the axis of advance. With the 315th Infantry Regiment attacking this sector frontally, the objective of 'Concentration 55 in Glaugny'[1] was assigned to the 313th. A group of two infantry companies and tanks attacked. However, the German reaction was brutal. The 1st Battalion of the 313th lost half of the men it had committed and even its headquarters, without managing to take the bridge at Glatigny and opening the way to Montgardon.

The "Guidon" is the traditional flag of American companies and battalions. With an infantry blue background, the one here is for the 1st Battalion of the 313th Infantry Regiment.

———

1. American maps read 'Glaugny' instead of Glatigny, the 't' and the 'i' being smudged into a 'u' when reproducing an older French army map.

THE JUNGLE AT MONT-CASTRE

The G-2 (intelligence) summary of the VIII US Corps headquarters for 7 July 1944 reports that, in the 90th Division zone, German paratroopers had been seen charging whilst shouting and firing their sub machine-guns. Indeed, in the thick forest of Mont-Castre, east of La Haye du Puits, the GI's were counter-attacked by Fallschirmjäger-Regiment 15. For five days, and despite the artillery fire, the paras led by Oberstleutnant Kurt Gröschke infiltrated the 'jungle' of Mont-Castre and got around the American positions to attack them from the rear.

This belt, belonging to a German paratrooper named 'Kern' of FJR 15, was found in the forest of Mont Castre. It was nicked by a shell splinter.

JIM FLOWERS

On 10 July, the 90th Division regained the upper hand at Camp de César, attacking the last positions of FJR 15 dug-in at the edge of the forest of Mont Castre. When a battalion of the 358th Infantry found itself almost surrounded, 2nd Lt. James (Jim) Franklin Flowers, commanding the first platoon of Company C, 712th Tank Battalion, obtained permission to rescue the cut-off battalion. He reached Colonel Bealke and his men, then decided to press on his attack. In the lead tank, with three others following and with an infantry company in support, Flowers pushed the German paratroopers back to the edge of the wood. Beyond the road to Lastelle, the tanks crossed a field and attacked machine-gun positions. Thinking that he was aligned with the unit to his right, Flowers halted in order to wait for the infantry. At that moment, his tank was hit from the left, and again, this time from the right, in the ammunition locker. The Sherman was on fire and Flowers gave the order to bail out. He could feel that he had been wounded but sought first to save his crew. He helped the gunner to get out but could not find the loader! Jumping out of the tank, Flowers realised that he had lost his right foot... Helped by the driver, they reached a hedge. During this time, German paratroopers knocked out the other tanks. Jim made a tourniquet with his belt and tightened it around his leg. The survivors defended themselves with pistols, carbines and sub machine-guns. Realising that the infantry was not coming, 2nd Lt. Flowers ordered those who could still walk to fall back. He remained alone with his seriously burnt gunner and an infantryman who had been hit in the legs. A German medic came to dress Jim and the gunner's hands, checked the tourniquet but refused to give them any water and ignored the infantryman. Early in the morning, they witnessed a German patrol passing by, then a platoon which began digging trenches. Almost immediately, an artillery barrage fell. Both the Germans and Americans were terrified. A splinter sheared off Jim's left leg and another hit the infantryman again in the leg. Jim made himself another tourniquet as well as one for the other soldier. During the afternoon of the 12th, the infantryman died in Jim's arms. The Germans had pulled back and Lieutenant Lovett of the 357th found Flowers. With both legs amputated, James Flowers never saw himself as being handicapped. For he had, as the surgeon said in 1944, "the will to live." Jim Flowers died in 2002 at the age of 88.

These crushed 75 mm shell cases were found by Henri Levaufre near the original position of Jim Flowers' tank at the foot of Mont Castre. Henri, a distinguished historian of the 90th Division and personal friend of Jim Flowers, was the one responsible, amongst other things, for the reunion between Flowers and the surgeon of the 344th Field Artillery Battalion who operated on him, Captain WM McConahey.

---

1. *From* 13 ans en 1944, nous étions tous en Normandie, by Henri Levaufre, *Eurocibles*, 2013.

GÖTZ VON BERLICHINGEN

Following their 13 June counter-attack at Carentan, Fallschirmjäger-Regiment 6 and the 17. SS-Panzer-Grenadier Division took up positions in front of Sainteny, blocking the narrow strip of land between the Gorges marshes and Carentan. On 9 July, Sainteny, devastated by artillery fire, fell after six days of violent combat. Despite losses of 5,000 men, the 83rd US Infantry Division, supported by the 4th, did not manage to reach either Périers or the Saint-Lô road. Even down to half of their strength on 25 July, the grenadiers of the 17.SS "Götz von Berlichingen" Div. were still fighting over the bank of the river Taute.

This motorbike pannier bearing the 'Iron Fist' insignia of the 17th SS Division was discovered at Saint-Martin de Cenilly in 2013, in the Roncey Pocket, where a great many of this unit's vehicles were abandoned.

THE SPEARHEAD CANNOT GET THROUGH

On 11 July between Saint-Jean-de-Daye and Pont-Hébert, the Americans lost the opportunity of breaching the entire frontline west of Saint-Lô. The Vire-Taute canal and the Vire were crossed relatively easily and the 30th US Infantry Division entered into the German lines. However, the staff of the XIX Corps improvised the exploitation and hurriedly tried to "push an elephant through a mouse hole". A hundred tanks of the 3rd US Armored Division jammed the small roads and could not move. Elements of the 17th SS Division, Schnelle-Brigade 30 and tanks of the 2. Panzer-SS halted them for five days, before being joined by the Panzer-Lehr Division.

This tread from a Sherman tank's road wheel was found in front of the high ground of Hauts-Vents, the intermediate objective of the Pont-Hébert breakthrough.

3. FALLSCHIRMJÄGER -DIVISION

Put on alert on 6 June, the
3. Fallschirmjäger-Division (3. FJD)
left Brittany the following day. Covering
350 kilometres to the east of Saint-Lô in
eight or ten days of route marching, the
last parachutists of General Schimpf arrived
in Cerisy forest during the night of 17-18
June. On 21 June, they held a line more than
twenty kilometres long. With the Americans
concentrating their efforts on Cherbourg, the
attacks were limited. However, on 11 July,
when the 2nd US Infantry Division engaged
two regiments at Hill 192 and towards
the Bayeux road, they had to dislodge
the German paras huddled behind their
machine-guns and mortars. As the GI's said
themselves with admiration, the German
parachutists did not surrender, they died in
their foxholes.

This German MP40 sub machine-gun was
found at Hamel, near Condé-sur-Vire, where
the 3rd Parachute Division HQ was located
during the battle of Saint-Lô. The weapon
has been camouflaged with green paint.
In Normandy, the Fallschirmjäger and in
particular those of Schimpf, earned the
reputation of being masters of camouflage.

THE RANGERS AT HILL 192

Despite their difficulties on the beaches, the units which landed at Omaha Beach advanced more rapidly than the others on the Normandy front. In one week, the 1st US Infantry Division was in front of Caumont-l'Eventé and the 29th and 2nd Divisions found themselves before Saint-Lô. The attacks on this front, established in June, continued in July after the capture of Cherbourg.

These badges, given to a family at Cerisy-la-Forêt, are those of the 'Ranger Battle Training Course' [1]. This unofficial insignia showed that the bearer had taken part in an exercise involving approximately 150 infantrymen, artillerymen and engineers of the 2nd US Infantry Division at Camp McCoy, Wisconsin. These badges were made by the officers' wives and awarded at the end of the course on 5 June 1943.

---

1. From *Keep Up The Fire, The Ninth Infantry Regiment in WWII*, by Albaro L. Castillo, Southern Heritage Press, 2001.

HILL 122 AND LE CARILLON

Despite being well-trained, upon arriving between La Meauffe and Villiers-Fossard, the 35th US Infantry Division endured the tough hedgerow fighting. After being stalled for three days, the 14th of July saw a breakthrough along the Vire river and brought a regiment to the vicinity of the Pont-Hébert – Saint-Lô road and Hill 122. The next day, on the other flank, the reserve regiment was launched frontally against the objective. By midnight it was on the hill top. At Le Carillon in the centre, pitted against the third regiment, the Germans were overwhelmed on both sides. The following day two counter-attacks were repulsed. The Germans pulled back on the 17th and the gates to Saint-Lô opened.

These German medic's pouches were found at Saint-Georges-Montcocq, near Hill 122.

THE LONG WAY TO SAINT-LÔ

After holding the line in front of Saint-Lô for more than a month, the 29th US Infantry Division laboriously carried on the offensive on 11 July. Following five days of fruitless attacks, the unit seemed to be paralysed. Nevertheless, beneath the ridge at Martinville, two battalions of the 116th Infantry advanced and on the 16th, were a kilometre from Saint-Lô. Cut-off and under artillery and mortar fire, they were joined by Major Howie and his battalion. However, the GIs were exhausted and Howie was killed, with the capture of Saint-Lô slipping from the grasp of these valiant men. With Hill 122 captured, the road north was opened and it was the 115th Infantry, along with a motorised group (Task Force Cota), which entered into the town on 18 July 1944.

Jewell Humphries's helmet bears the round blue and grey insignia of the 29th Division, most of which is hidden by mud. Humphries served with the 3rd Battalion, 116th Infantry Regiment, that of Major Howie. The cxample of this illustrious sergeant illustrates the commitment of the 29th Division on its long trail towards Saint-Lô. Humphries, twice wounded in June, and decorated with the Bronze Star for saving a wounded comrade at Saint-André-de-l'Epine, did not see Saint-Lô. Badly wounded, he was taken away to hospital at the beginning of July. [1]

---

1. It was in order to honour his 3,000 men killed or wounded that General Gerhardt, commanding the 29th Division, wished for the body of Major Thomas D. Howie, the symbol of their courage, to enter into Saint-Lô with the first Americans.

THE BATTLES FOR CAEN

At the beginning of July, although he was still defending his strategy of pinning down the Germans with limited objective attacks, Montgomery found himself exposed as much to criticism as to the Panzers themselves!

Indeed, the actions in June, in order to be decisive, appeared to be over ambitious. Operation 'Perch,' a large pincer movement sweeping wide to the west at Tilly-sur-Seulles, ended up in a defensive withdrawal and bitter failure at Villers-Bocage. The crushing numerical superiority of 'Epsom' should have resulted in a bridgehead over the Odon and allowed a breakthrough beyond the Orne as far as the road to Falaise. But on 30 June, another attempt via the west became stuck at Hill 112.

Despite these tactical failures, this attritional form of warfare wore the Panzers down on the Caen front. Indeed, eleven out of the thirteen German armoured divisions were there. But, with Cherbourg captured and the American offensive towards the south launched, whatever the cost, the frontline had to be straightened out and Caen captured.

On the evening of 7 July, the Allied air forces dropped 2,600 tonnes of bombs on the gates of the city. At dawn on the 8th, three infantry divisions supported by artillery, including naval guns, and 250 American medium bombers, attacked the Norman capital. Operation 'Charnwood' forced the Germans to withdraw but they only gave up the left bank and held on in the southern area of the city, behind the destroyed bridges.

Caen, the main objective on D-Day, was belatedly taken – albeit partially – on 9 July. The question then arose of a subsidiary operation in Brittany. However, the staff officers could see that they lacked the means, and the experience of Caen showed how well a massive attack could work when supported by large numbers of aircraft.

Two large-scale operations were then planned and implemented, one in the British sector, the other in the American. Led by three armoured divisions advancing behind a curtain of 8,000 tonnes of bombs east of the Orne on 20 July, the British 'Goodwood' offensive only led to the capture of the southern parts of Caen. A third of the British tanks were knocked out and the road to Falaise remained closed.

Even though it was Bradley who succeeded in this 'Blitzkrieg in reverse,' Montgomery claimed another strategic success. He had pinned down the enemy to the east and the Americans would be able to launch their offensive in the west through a moderately reinforced front.

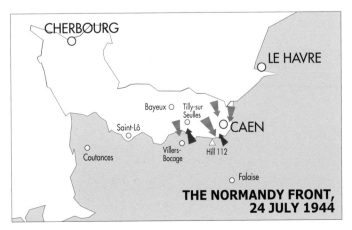

CHERBOURG

LE HAVRE

Bayeux   Tilly-sur Seulles

Saint-Lô   CAEN

Coutances   Villers-Bocage   Hill 112

Falaise

THE NORMANDY FRONT, 24 JULY 1944

21. PANZERDIVISION

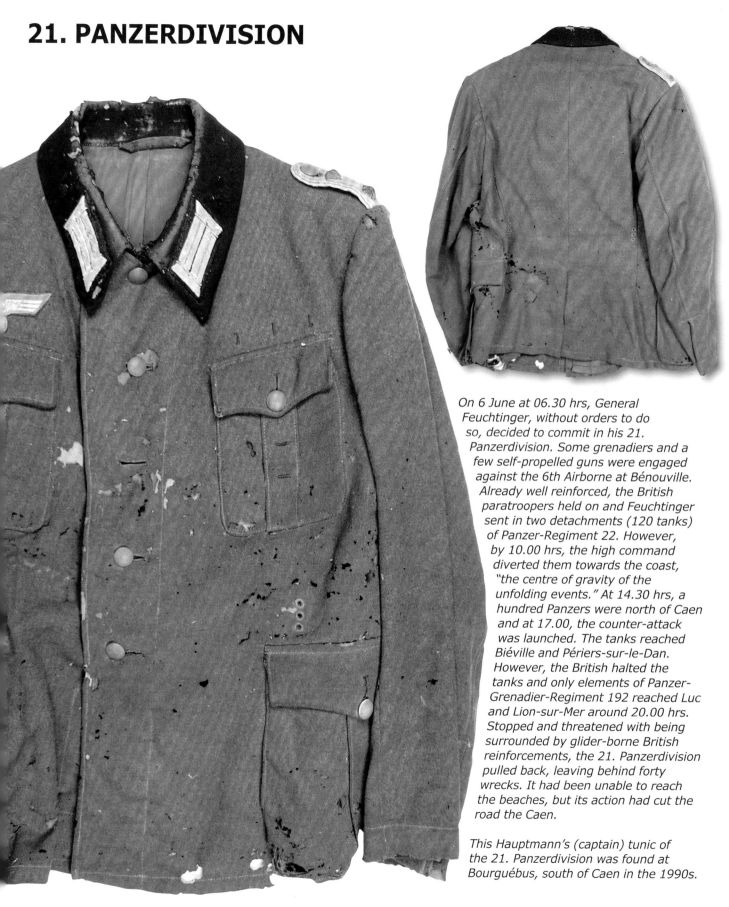

On 6 June at 06.30 hrs, General Feuchtinger, without orders to do so, decided to commit in his 21. Panzerdivision. Some grenadiers and a few self-propelled guns were engaged against the 6th Airborne at Bénouville. Already well reinforced, the British paratroopers held on and Feuchtinger sent in two detachments (120 tanks) of Panzer-Regiment 22. However, by 10.00 hrs, the high command diverted them towards the coast, "the centre of gravity of the unfolding events." At 14.30 hrs, a hundred Panzers were north of Caen and at 17.00, the counter-attack was launched. The tanks reached Biéville and Périers-sur-le-Dan. However, the British halted the tanks and only elements of Panzer-Grenadier-Regiment 192 reached Luc and Lion-sur-Mer around 20.00 hrs. Stopped and threatened with being surrounded by glider-borne British reinforcements, the 21. Panzerdivision pulled back, leaving behind forty wrecks. It had been unable to reach the beaches, but its action had cut the road the Caen.

This Hauptmann's (captain) tunic of the 21. Panzerdivision was found at Bourguébus, south of Caen in the 1990s.

DESERT RATS AT VILLERS-BOCAGE

Operation 'Perch' on 13 June brought a column of the 7th British Armoured Division to Villers-Bocage. At Eight in the morning, the 22nd Armoured Brigade was in the town itself and the leading elements left to reconnoitre Hill 213. At 08.30 hrs, a Tiger tank commanded by Obersturmführer Michael Wittmann burst onto the road. Three British tanks were destroyed and, along with two other Tigers, Wittmann drove along the column, reaping devastation. At 9 o'clock, more Tigers attacked, joined by grenadiers and Panzer IV tanks. By 18.00 hrs, the British had lost 26 tanks and thirty armoured vehicles, but six of the thirteen Tigers, including Wittmann's, had been stopped.

This divisional sign from General Erskine's 7th British Armoured Division was found in Caen city centre.

CHARGING BULL

The British 'Epsom' operation strove to jump over the Odon river, cross the Orne and position tanks south of Caen on the Falaise road. However, on 30 June, after five days of fighting on the Odon and at Hill 112, the 11th Armoured Division left the arena and carried out its strategic withdrawal via the bridge at Mondrainville. The latter could only support one Sherman at a time and withdrawing 300 vehicles in one night under driving rain was a small victory in itself. Countered and threatened by the Panzers of two SS armoured corps, the outclassed British tanks left to reinforce a deep defensive line. Attritional warfare began in front of Hill 112.

This steel helmet decorated with the charging bull insignia of the 11th Armoured Division was given to a Norman by a veteran of this unit.

HITLERJUGEND

On the afternoon of 7 June, young soldiers of the SS "Hitlerjugend" Division attacked a Canadian column that was probing towards Carpiquet. They recaptured Authie and Franqueville but were stopped in front of Buron. On 8 June at Norrey-en-Bessin, the Regina Rifles (3rd Canadian Division) fought back and prevented SS-Panzergrenadier-Regiment 26 from cutting them off from the British. At Putot-en-Bessin, the Royal Winnipeg Rifles were violently forced out but the Canadian Scottish re-took the village. On the evening of the 8th, Kurt Meyer[1] launched a Panther attack against Rots. However, after a night of fighting, the SS had to pull back. The Canadians had set up strong defensive positions and the battle began again in a series of limited attacks, such as at Mesnil-Patry and again at Rots on 11 June. Fighting resumed against the 'Scottish Corridor' held by the 15th (Scottish) Infantry Division, who had opened a route for the tanks towards the Odon. Finally, on 5 July, the North Shore and the Chaudières pushed the SS grenadiers out of Carpiquet in hand to hand fighting. However, the Winnipeg Rifles still did not manage to take the airfield. The battle of Caen had begun.

This steel helmet with its specific Waffen-SS camouflage cover was found on the west bank of the river Seine.

---

1. On 14 June, Kurt Meyer, the CO of SS-Panzergrenadier-Regiment 25, took command of the 12. SS-Panzer-Division 'Hitlerjugend,' following the death of Kommandeur Witt in a bombardment at the divisional HQ at Venoix, a northern borough of Caen.

MAJOR GORDON BROWN

At Authie on 8 July, when his Dog Company joined him at 18.00 hrs, Brown had lost his supporting tanks and the artillery preparation was over. However, the Major left with two other companies of the Regina Rifles (3rd Can. Div.) to attack Ardenne abbey, the HQ of the Hitlerjugend division. Baker Company rushed into the forward positions and lost half of its strength. Charlie and Dog Companies advanced with difficulty under tracer fire. The machine-guns prevented any approach and Brown requested artillery support. Towards 21.00, the advance resumed. Before the final rush, the mortars fired their smoke bombs and Brown leapt out of the wheat and dust with two platoons. Firing all of their weapons and throwing grenades into the last trenches, the Canadians reached the abbey [1]. Brown would be able to enjoy the cherries 'Panzermeyer' had left in his room !

These boots and cinema ticket were Gordon Brown's lucky charms. He kept the cinema ticket in his pocket and only took off his boots to change his socks. In October 1944, the battalion cobbler had to remove the leggings of his worn out assault boots and fit them to new boots...

---

1. Major (Douglas) Gordon Brown was decorated with the Distinguished Service Order (DSO).

IN THE RUINS

On 7 July 1944, from 21.50 to 22.30 hrs, 460 Royal Air Force aircraft dropped 2,600 tonnes of bombs on the northern suburbs of Caen. The Allies had decided to use for the first time heavy bombers in the role of tactical support for a ground operation. However, although the effect on the German defences cannot be denied, at least 300 civilians were killed, adding to those already killed in June. At the end of the operations in Normandy, two thousand of Caen's citizens had been killed by the bombing raids.

This French helmet, found in a Caen cellar, was painted white for the civil defence teams, and is a reminder of those men and women who braved the dangers of the ruins to help the victims of the bombing raids.

TO DIE FOR CAEN

At 04.30 hrs on 8 July 1944, Operation 'Charnwood' began with 5,000 infantrymen on the road to Caen, supported by 500 tanks, 600 artillery pieces and four Royal Navy battleships. The advance was slow and it was not until the 9th that a patrol reached the borough of Saint-Julien, making its way slowly through the bomb craters. To the west, the 17th Duke of York's Royal Canadian Hussars, the reconnaissance unit of the 3rd Canadian Division, tried to seize a bridge over the Orne.

Canadian Trooper Anselm John MacDonald, of the 17th Duke of York's, was killed on 9 July 1944. His kit bag was found south of Caen in 2004.

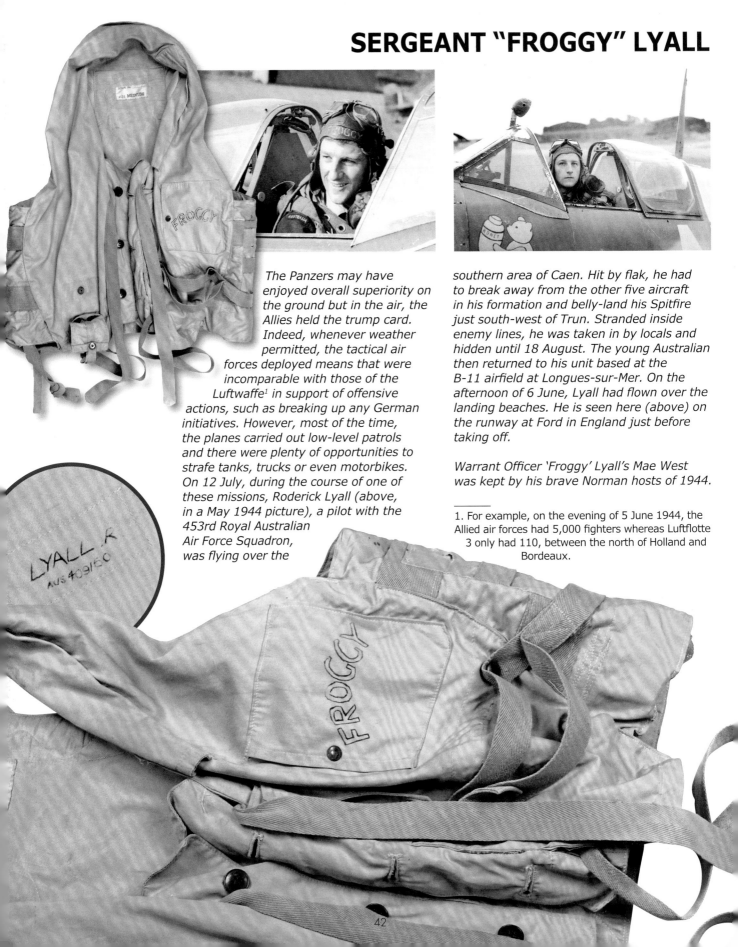

SERGEANT "FROGGY" LYALL

The Panzers may have enjoyed overall superiority on the ground but in the air, the Allies held the trump card. Indeed, whenever weather permitted, the tactical air forces deployed means that were incomparable with those of the Luftwaffe[1] in support of offensive actions, such as breaking up any German initiatives. However, most of the time, the planes carried out low-level patrols and there were plenty of opportunities to strafe tanks, trucks or even motorbikes. On 12 July, during the course of one of these missions, Roderick Lyall (above, in a May 1944 picture), a pilot with the 453rd Royal Australian Air Force Squadron, was flying over the southern area of Caen. Hit by flak, he had to break away from the other five aircraft in his formation and belly-land his Spitfire just south-west of Trun. Stranded inside enemy lines, he was taken in by locals and hidden until 18 August. The young Australian then returned to his unit based at the B-11 airfield at Longues-sur-Mer. On the afternoon of 6 June, Lyall had flown over the landing beaches. He is seen here (above) on the runway at Ford in England just before taking off.

Warrant Officer 'Froggy' Lyall's Mae West was kept by his brave Norman hosts of 1944.

---

1. For example, on the evening of 5 June 1944, the Allied air forces had 5,000 fighters whereas Luftflotte 3 only had 110, between the north of Holland and Bordeaux.

OPERATION GOODWOOD

Despite the effect of surprise caused by this new offensive and the 5 kilometre leap forward achieved in the morning, by midday on 18 July, the British advance had stopped. The tanks of three British divisions were counter-attacked by three Panzer divisions. The final efforts of 19 and 20 July came to nothing. 'Goodwood,' which was supposed to shatter the front, ended in the mud of a storm and at the price of 4,000 men and 500 tanks lost.

This sign was found at Cuverville in 2012. On the morning of 18 July 1944, it pointed the way of the "Briar" route east of the Orne, reserved for vehicles of the 11th British Armoured Division up to their start positions.

SERGEANT BENOIT LACOURSE

After 'Goodwood,' Montgomery wanted to keep up the pressure on the Germans south of Caen. On 23 July, the Régiment de Maisonneuve (2nd Canadian Division) received the order to take Etavaux. Sergeant Lacourse was in command of No 15 platoon/ C Company. Pinned down in front of the village by machine-gun fire coming from the right, Lacourse's men, except for four, slipped to the left with the neighbouring platoon. Then he boldly led his men and rushed the machine-guns, knocking out three with grenades.

This paybook and identity tag belonged to Sergeant Benoit Lacourse, decorated with the Distinguished Conduct Medal for his actions at Etavaux.

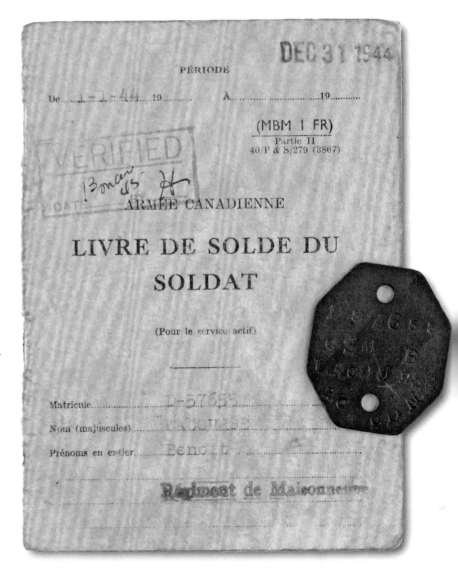

'COBRA'

For Montgomery, the Americans were now ready to launch their right hook by breaking through along the west coast of the Cotentin, pushing through via Avranches then pivot towards the east in order to encircle the Germans pinned down on the Caen front, whilst at the same time protecting an army that would advance into Brittany.

But the intermediate objective of Operation 'Cobra' remained Coutances. South of the Lessay - Saint-Lô road, the hedgerows seemed to be less dense than along the line of marshes. There were more roads and these were also wider and often tarmacked, thus allowing tanks to be engaged and put some impetus into the advance. As was now routine procedure, the attack would only go in following 'carpet bombing.'

Thus on 25 July, 2,500 bombers crushed a sector some seven kilometres wide west of Saint-Lô. The infantry went in on the 26th against Marigny and Saint-Gilles to keep open the breach through which the mechanised force would drive towards Coutances, protected in the south by an armoured division.

However, the manoeuvre did not find the right tempo and the enemy rapidly pulled back along the coast. Seeing that the Germans would not be encircled north of Coutances, General Collins changed his plan. He sent tanks towards Lengronne in order to cut off the road to the Germans further south. By isolating 7,000 Waffen-SS and paratroopers in the Roncey Pocket, the Americans trapped the better enemy elements that had been acting as a shield to enable a general withdrawal.

The German command, baffled by the assassination attempt on Hitler on 20 July, fooled by a diversionary attack led by the Canadians, and deprived of its main armoured force crushed beneath the bombs, did not know how to react. The retreat had started and a new line of defence envisaged at Avranches.

However, on 31 July, the Americans already held the bridge at Pontaubault. Two armoured divisions were at the gates of Brittany. At the beginning of August, Patton, "the best American soldier", according to the Germans, continued his charge in the finest traditions of the cavalry, pushing his tanks and forcing the Germans to withdraw inside the coastal fortresses. In the east, other units were moving towards Laval and Le Mans. The encirclement of the German armies west of the Seine was almost complete and Paris seemed within reach.

**THE WESTERN FRONT
7 AUGUST 1944**

RHINO TO THE RESCUE

Since the beginning of the battle, the Allied tanks had been unable to break through the solid hedgerows of the Normandy 'Bocage.' However, on 25 July, three out of five American tanks engaged in the 'Cobra' breakthrough had been fitted with special devices, which Bradley had kept secret until the offensive. One of these was a set of ploughshares welded on the hull front. Driving at full power towards the obstacle, the tank would not rear up and would then be able to uproot the hedgerow.

This 'Rhino horn' was found along with others in a meadow near Méautis. It was locally made by American mechanics using metal beams from recovered German beach obstacles.

THE END OF THE PANZER-LEHR

On 25 July, 1,500 heavy and 1,000 medium bombers dropped over 4,000 tonnes of high explosive, fragmentation and incendiary bombs across a sector including Montreuil-sur-Lozon, La Chapelle-en-Juger and Hébécrevon. They blasted the Panzer-Lehr Division and its attached units. Losses were over 2,000 men, a third of the German troops on the lines west of Saint-Lô. Other air raids prevented all reorganisation in the German rear areas. Fritz Bayerlein sent a report to his superiors stating that his division had ceased to function as a fighting unit.

These spare track links, stored on the side of a Panther tank turret, were found west of Hébécrevon, just below the Périers – Saint-Lô road. The red Roman number I identifies a tank of HQ company, I./Panzer-Regiment 6., the Panther battalion of the Panzer-Lehr Division in Normandy.

MARIGNY TO SAINT-GILLES

Marching behind the curtain of bombs, the assault troops and sappers attacked the crossroads and strategic high ground. In order to protect the tanks' axis of progression, elements of the 9th and 30th US Infantry Divisions had to lay down a curtain of defensive fire on either side of the breach from the Périers - Saint-Lô road and up to Marigny and Saint-

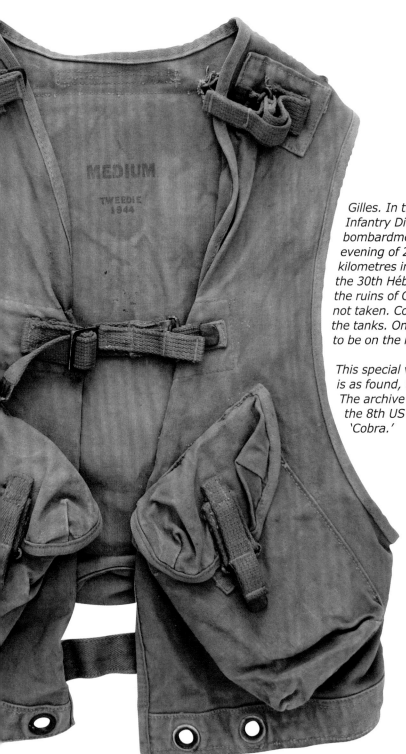

Gilles. In the centre, two battalions of the 8th Infantry (4th US Infantry Division) were tasked with mopping-up. Despite the bombardment, the enemy put up unexpected resistance. On the evening of 25 July, the American penetration was rarely over two kilometres in depth. The 9th Division held Montreuil-sur-Lozon, the 30th Hébécrevon and the soldiers of the 4th surrounded the ruins of Chapelle-en-Juger. Marigny and Saint-Gilles were not taken. Collins hesitated but finally took the risk of sending in the tanks. On the evening of the 25th, the Shermans were alerted to be on the move for the following morning.

This special vest, issued to American assault troops for 6 June, is as found, the lower part and its large pockets being cut-off. The archive photo shows that this was common practice within the 8th US Infantry Regiment at the beginning of Operation 'Cobra.'

'HELL ON WHEELS'

Collins feared traffic jams and only committed two motorised columns on the 26th. General Huebner's 1st Division was tasked with securing Marigny then pursuing the advance as soon as possible towards Coutances, supported by tanks. Combat Command A of the US 2nd Armored Division ('Hell on Wheels') took Saint-Gilles and set up positions which would allow them to deal with a counter-attack from the south-east, where the largest German units were situated.

This crash helmet bearing the Tank Destroyers insignia was found at Villebaudon. In its advance towards Saint-Gilles, Canisy, Saint-Samson de Bonfossé, Le Mesnil-Herman and Villebaudon, CCA of the 2nd US Armored Division was protected by A and B Companies of the 702nd Tank Destroyer Battalion, armed with self-propelled anti-tank guns.

MAINTAINING CONTACT

On 26 July, the VIII US Corps units between Lessay and Périers attacked. The main push was aimed at the centre, and delivered by the 8th US Infantry Division. The idea was to advance as far as Geffosses, Saint-Sauveur-Lendelin and Marigny, then maintaining contact with the enemy in order to give enough time for Huebner's column to carry out its manoeuvre. There was determined German resistance on the 26th, but early the next day, the Americans were only held up by thick minefields which had been laid during the night by the Germans to cover their withdrawal. The 'Monthuchon Pocket' which Collins had hoped to achieve was never formed.

This haversack belonging to an infantryman of the 28th Infantry Regiment (8th US Infantry Division) was found at the end of the division's course in Brittany, on the Crozon peninsula opposite Brest. The divisional insignia has been drawn in ink on the flap.

THE RONCEY POCKET

Sent in on 27 July, CCB of the 2nd US Armored Division was given the star role. The attempts by the 1st Infantry Division and the 3rd Armored Division to cut-off the Germans at Coutances failed and by driving hard towards Bréhal, the 2nd AD was the last chance to stop them. On the morning of the 28th, the CCB had reached Notre-Dame de Cenilly and received the order to halt at Lengronne, to set up positions and to hold or destroy the bridges over the Sienne. To the west, the Germans continued to withdraw, but at Montpinchon and Roncey, elements of the 17.SS-Panzergrenadier and 2.SS-Panzer Divisions and the paratroopers of Fallschirmjäger-Regiment 6 were trapped. On 28 July, Obersturmbannführer Tychsen, commander of the 2.SS, was killed at Trelly. Before dawn on the 29th, the Germans attempted to break out at Saint-Martin and Notre-Dame de Cenilly. That same day, artillery and tactical aviation destroyed no less than 350 vehicles blocked around Roncey. During the night of the 29th, two columns escaped via Saint-Denis le Gast, but a larger third column was destroyed at the well-named Lande des Morts [1] (Dead man's moor).

This Waffen-SS greatcoat was found at Saint-Martin de Cenilly. The badge under the collar is an American marksman's award. Its similar shape to an Iron Cross is probably the reason it was pinned on by the German owner of the coat.

1. His unit under attack, Sergeant Hulon B. Whittington of the 41st Armored Infantry Regiment jumped onto a tank and guided it towards the front of the German column. Knocking out the first vehicle blocked the rest of the file. The battle raged for six hours. Whittington was awarded the Medal of Honor, the highest American military award, for his actions at the Lande des Morts.

WHAT WAR IS ALL ABOUT

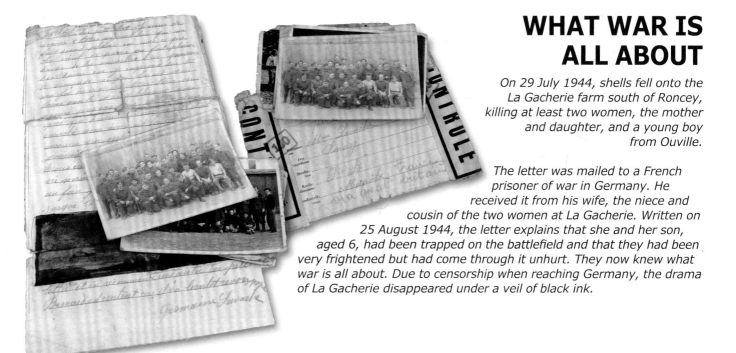

On 29 July 1944, shells fell onto the La Gacherie farm south of Roncey, killing at least two women, the mother and daughter, and a young boy from Ouville.

The letter was mailed to a French prisoner of war in Germany. He received it from his wife, the niece and cousin of the two women at La Gacherie. Written on 25 August 1944, the letter explains that she and her son, aged 6, had been trapped on the battlefield and that they had been very frightened but had come through it unhurt. They now knew what war is all about. Due to censorship when reaching Germany, the drama of La Gacherie disappeared under a veil of black ink.

THE RACE IS ON

On 30 July, the pursuit got underway. The two American army corps which had diverted German forces away in the east during 'Cobra' were now at the gates of Vire. The Germans had to resist here, for, without this key position, they would lose all hope of closing the front around Avranches. Sensing a vacuum under the frontline at Vire, Collins sent the 3rd US Armored Division towards Villedieu-les-Poêles. However, the move lacked impetus

so Collins attached the two armoured Combat Commands to the 4th and 1st US Infantry Divisions. On 31 July, the Americans had driven through Brécey onto Mortain.

This sign indicating an aid post was found at Saint-Denis-le-Vêtu in 2004. The code name of 'Oxford' identifies the 45th Armored Medical Battalion of the 3rd US Armored Division.

CRUSHED BY THE 'SUPER SIXTH'

Starting from Périers, the 4th US Armored Division took Coutances on 28 July. The next day, the 6th Armored Division drove hard as far as the Roque bridge whilst the bridges at Cérences and Ver, also out, stopped the 4th. On 30 July, the engineers enabled the tanks to continue their thrust and the 4th succeeded in breaking out at Avranches. Confined on the sole road leading south and thus vulnerable, the Americans continued their effort, despite a German counter-attack. On 1 August, they had secured bridges over the river Sélune at Pontaubault and Ducey. A week later, the tanks of the "Super Sixth" has reached the outskirts of Brest.

This German water bottle, crushed by a column of the 6th US Armored Division, was found on the road side at Bourg-Blanc, north of Brest.

VALUABLE ASSISTANCE

Although the Jedburgh or SAS[1] helped in coordinating of the action of the French Résistance, a determining element arrived along with Patton's headquarters. Integrated into the G-3 staff section of the 3rd US Army, the 11th Special Force Detachment was mainly tasked with guiding the action of the Forces Françaises de l'Intérieur (FFI) in support of military operations. The order for Brittany stated that the FFI had to protect the flanks of American units and mop-up the smallest enemy forces. The Breton Resistance fighters went on to show great efficiency in fighting alongside Patton's troops.[2]

1. Jedburgh missions were carried out by two officers and a radio operator, usually a Frenchman, an American and a British soldier.
2. From the 11th Special Force Detachment Operations Report, Lt. Col. Robert I. Powell.

This German belt buckle, which has been "de-Nazified", belonged to a Resistance member from Cloître-Saint-Thégonnec, near Morlaix.

WITHDRAWAL TO BREST

The fighting in the Cotentin had absorbed about two thirds of the German troops garrisoned in Brittany, so the conquest of the latter was envisioned as a very open exploitation where three armoured forces would cut off the peninsula, protect the Rennes – Brest railway line and capture the ports. On 1 August 1944, the Americans were delayed by a few detachments withdrawn from Normandy and parachutists of the 2. Fallschirmjäger-Division were sent from the Brest sector. When these Germans encountered American tanks on 5 August, these were already close to Huelgoat and Carhaix. Outflanked by the Resistance (fighting alongside the 6th US Armored Division) in the thick woods, they broke through and withdrew towards Brest. There, pitted against strong fortifications, the American armour awaited infantry support as they also did at Lorient and Saint-Nazaire. But most infantry units had been sucked in by the advance north of the Loire. At Saint-Malo, another fortress, the fighting that had begun on 5 August lasted for nearly a month and the attack at Brest did not resume until the end of the month.

This German parachutist helmet and its specific cover were found near Quimper (after having been thrown into a skip at a dump!) in the 2000s.

FAILURE AT MORTAIN

Whereas the Allies were hoping for a German rout towards the Seine, Hitler was thinking of the exact opposite. The Americans had indeed broken through, but their base was vulnerable, their flanks open and the Brittany ports still in German hands....

Hitler wanted to counter-attack from Mortain, convinced that he could cut-off the American armies in half at

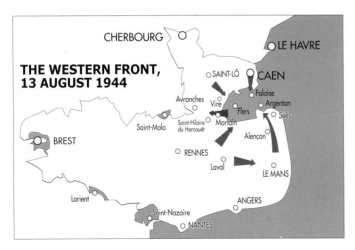

Avranches, sweep round the Allied front and push everyone back into the sea!

The men at the front did not really believe in winning back the ground that had been lost, but they saw that by holding a defensive line back at Avranches, they might be able to return to static warfare and prepare for the inevitable withdrawal.

The surprise attack was launched in the early hours of 7 August, and main thrust penetrated ten kilometres west of Mortain. In the South, the Saint-Hilaire-du-Harcouët road appeared to be open. However, once daylight came, the German tanks were crushed by the artillery and the fighter-bombers. As for the German aircraft, they did not turn up.

For the German staff, the only option was that of retreat, but Hitler ordered the attack to continue. Two armoured divisions brought in from the Caen front were to go into action towards Avranches. However, the Canadian offensive of 8 August towards Falaise and the threat to Alençon prevented reinforcements from being allotted to the counter-attack. It was now the Americans' turn to advance in the Mortain salient.

What was now paramount for the Germans was the need to stem Patton's advance. On 11 August, the panzers left Mortain in order to head towards Alençon.

Caught out by the speed of the Americans and the French 2e Division Blindée of Gen. Leclerc, which captured Alençon and Sées on 12 August, the armoured group withdrawn from Mortain did not attack here either. In a precarious position when defending La Ferté-Macé, Carrouges, Ecouché and Argentan, it was ordered to escape towards the east before it was too late.

ENTER THE GUARDS

The American breakthrough in the west and the fixation of the Panzers south of Caen spurred Montgomery into launching British units in the middle. On 30 July, Operation 'Bluecoat' lined up six divisions towards a line from Vire to Flers and three Guards[1] formations were engaged. Thus, the 6th Guards Tank Brigade, 2nd Household Cavalry Regiment and the Guards Armoured Division supported the British VIII Corps in the main effort from Caumont-l'Eventé towards Vire. The British succeeded in breaking through beyond Saint-Martin-des-Besaces and crossing the Souleuvre, but on approaching Vire, they came up against the extremity of the German front which had been bolstered prior to the Mortain counter-attack.

These souvenirs were found together. The embroidered shoulder titles of two Guards regiments were placed under the helmet's camouflage netting.

---

1. The 6th Guards Tank Brigade (heavy armoured brigade) comprised of Grenadier, Coldstream and Scots Guards. The 2nd Household Cavalry Regiment (reconnaissance) comprised of the Life Guards and Royal Horse Guards. The Guards Armoured Division comprised of Welsh, Grenadier, Coldstream and Irish Guards.

MAYENNE, 5 AUGUST 1944

On 2 August, the German front to the west of the Saint-Sever forest had shrunk, and due to the jam within the Avranches corridor, the course of operations changed. When the 79th and 90th US Infantry Divisions, on the left flank of the advance towards Brittany, became liable to break through at Saint-Hilaire-du-Harcouët and Fougères, Patton accepted the challenge of a rapid charge towards the south-east. On 5 August, the 90th captured Mayenne. On the 6th at Laval, the 79th opened up the road to Le Mans and elements of the 90th were near Sainte-Suzanne. With their supply bases at Alençon and Le Mans under threat, the Germans would speed up their operation 'Lüttich.'

This German helmet has survived with its period label which translates as "Mayenne – Liberation of 5 August 1944 – German helmet picked up in town".

OPERATION LÜTTICH

On 7 July just after midnight, the 2. Panzerdivision created a surprise and broke through to the west of Mesnil-Adelée, five kilometres from the objective, the road from Brécey to Saint-Hilaire-du-Harcouët. This was the first spearhead of an attack with three divisions, followed closely by a fourth which had to drive towards Avranches. Another column of the 2. Panzer found itself stalled in front of Juvigny-le-Tertre. The momentum was lost. Even if the 1. SS-Panzerdivision, held in reserve and planned for the exploitation phase, was launched through the lines held by the 2. Panzer, the advance did not get underway. In the North, the 116. Panzer did not make any progress either. The attacks were delivered on narrow fronts and the tanks rapidly jammed the roads. When day came, the Allied aircraft, much feared by the Germans, came into action. In the morning, the American artillery also came into play and the last German hopes were wiped out. At midday, the order was given to halt the attack. Operation Lüttich[1] had just failed.

This armour plate is one of the two rear doors of a SdKfz 251 (Sonderkraftfahrzeug 251) half-track. The trident tactical marking is that of the 2. Panzerdivision. The period photograph was taken about ten days later in Chambois.

---

1. Lüttich (Liege) was the name chosen for the operation and was a reminder of a German victory in August 1914.

THE BREACH AT SAINT-HILAIRE

On the morning of 7 August, on the southern flank of the Lüttich counter-offensive, elements of the 2.SS-Panzer-Division and 17.SS-Panzergrenadier-Division managed to slip around both sides of Mortain. They reached the high ground at Romagny to the west and took up good positions along the road to Saint-Hilaire-du-Harcouët. When the attack stopped, they were mid-way to Avranches and only the artillery had impeded them. Hitler was furious when reports came in confirming the failure. He was convinced that his counter-attack could have succeeded with the means that he had planned. At the front, the staff officers had rushed into the attack and had not known how to react. The Führer did not understand how the SS

armoured division allocated for the exploitation phase had been thrown into the fray when it should have gone into the breach at Saint-Hilaire. In the afternoon of 7 August, he issued an order to transfer the three Panzer divisions from the Vire to Caen front and to pursue the attack "with audacity and temerity as far as the sea."

This Mauser K98k rifle, a special issue for the Waffen-SS (hence the various death's heads and runic markings), was found south of Romagny on the Mortain – Saint-Hilaire-du-Harcouët road. The fact that its butt has been broken testifies to a common American practice concerning the immediate destruction of weapons after the capture of prisoners.

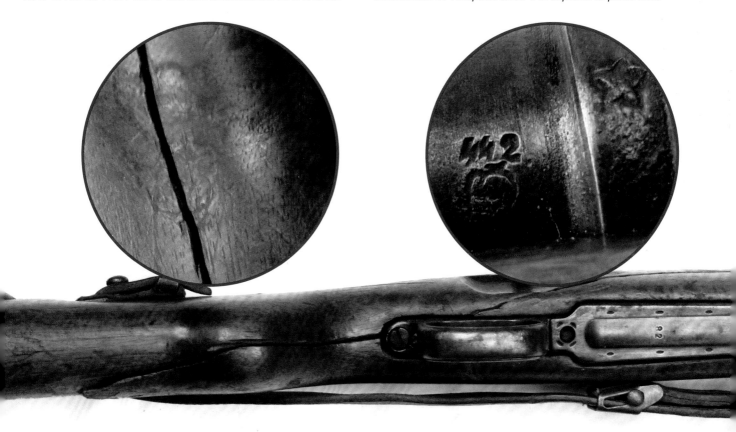

ROOSEVELT'S SS

During 'Lüttich,' the bulk of the Panzers broke through the lines held by the 30th US Infantry Division. At the outset of the attack, several units were surrounded on the hill east of Mortain and at Saint-Barthélemy. Even though the anti-tank guns and artillery stopped the enemy, the battle of Mortain would continue for another four days. The 30th Division suffered almost 2,000 casualties, 300 of which at least were from the lost battalion on Hill 317[1]. These men organised their defence around a few anti-tank guns and repulsed the repeated attacks of the SS grenadiers. This determination later earned them the nickname of 'Roosevelt's SS' from the German high command.

Found at Mesnillard, west of Mortain, this American bayonet belonged to Private Manus, of the engineer platoon of the 629th Tank Destroyer Battalion, attached to the 30th US Infantry Division during the Mortain fighting. His name, but above all the "aye" and the "aye want to go home" etched on the scabbard reveal his Scottish origins... and his homesickness.

––––––––
1. The men of the 2nd Battalion, 120th Infantry Regiment, easily managed to hold onto Hill 317 for two days. But, despite assistance from a few French farmers in the vicinity, the situation worsened. On 10 August, planes dropped supplies and ammunition. The same day, the artillery sent in field dressings and morphine in hollow shells.

THE 'SMALL PURSUIT' OF MORTAIN

While Panzergruppe Eberbach [1] prepared for a new attack, the Canadian offensive south of Caen and the American threat to Alençon cancelled out this last attempt to reach Avranches. During the night of 11 August, the Panzers pulled back from Mortain in order to face the Americans moving up from Le Mans towards Alençon. The attempt to encircle the Germans was now obvious. As early as the 12th, German resistance collapsed and the 'small pursuit' of Mortain began. The 2nd US Armored Division reached Domfront on 14 August. The next day, the 2nd and 29th US Infantry Divisions arrived from the north-west to capture Tinchebray. Flers was liberated on 16 August by tanks of the British 11th Armoured Division.

This pair of American 6x30 binoculars was found at St. Bômer les Forges, north-west of Domfront.

---

1. Following Hitler's order to recapture Avranches with six armoured divisions, General Eberbach took command of the Panzergruppe bearing his name and specially formed for the new offensive.

THE BATTLE OF RÂNES-FROMENTEL

The Americans and French approaching Argentan on 13 August, trailing columns of armoured vehicles in their wake, had formed the outline of a thin-walled pocket. In order to avoid a German break-out towards the south, the US VII Corps drove hard from Mayenne towards the main Flers – Argentan road. Between Rânes and the Fromentel crossroads, the Americans had to fight for five days in the face of a determined defence from elements of the Eberbach group and other units, including some paratroopers who were beginning their retreat to the east.

This German parachutist qualification badge was found between Rânes and Joué-du-Bois. It was the result of a swap between two civilians. A young man who had taken weapons to the Gendarmerie at Rânes just after the fighting was rewarded with cigarettes, which he then immediately swapped for two 'desirable' German badges.

THE FALAISE CAULDRON

Now south of Argentan, the Americans hoped to encircle the enemy by driving hard towards Falaise, but the order did not come. On 14 August instead, some of their forces departed for the Seine river.

On the same day, two Canadian armoured columns heralded by heavy bombers conquered Falaise at last. On 17 August, the Canadians were some 25 kilometres distant from Argentan and the Americans. A large pocket had formed in the west, as far as Flers.

On 16 August, the threat posed by the closure of the pocket and the landings in Southern France compelled the German high command to decide for a general withdrawal to the Seine and Yonne rivers, and as far as the Swiss border.

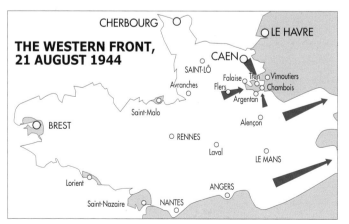

THE WESTERN FRONT, 21 AUGUST 1944

CHERBOURG
LE HAVRE
CAEN
SAINT-LÔ
Falaise · Trun · Vimoutiers
Avranches Flers · Chambois
Argentan
Saint-Malo
Alençon
BREST
RENNES
Laval
LE MANS
Lorient
ANGERS
Saint-Nazaire NANTES

Estimating that it would require three nights to pass the Orne and another to cross the Dives, the Germans would have to hold the 'neck' of the bag open for four days.

The Allies' priority, in turn, was to close the pocket. Launched east of Falaise on 17 August, two armoured divisions, one Canadian and the other Polish, reached Trun and Saint-Lambert the following day. On the 19th, the Poles pushed forward along two routes of advance. A detachment took the northern part of Hill 262 at Montormel and another headed into Chambois and found the Americans. The link-up had now taken place, but the pocket had not been closed. Further to the west, the British led two successful advances south of Falaise and north-east of Argentan.

Despite the lack of supplies and the constant artillery fire and air attacks, on 19 August, the bulk of the German troops had managed to withdraw behind the main Argentan – Falaise road. On 20 August, Germans paratroopers and armour attacked towards Saint-Lambert, Chambois and Montormel in order to open the escape route.

The Canadians hung on to Saint-Lambert; the Poles and Americans fought side-by-side in Chambois. At Montormel, the Poles were cut-off and could not stem the German withdrawal towards Vimoutiers. The Canadians reached them on the 21st and by the end of the afternoon, the Falaise Pocket was closed. The encircled troops, now only capable of pointless combat in the midst of destroyed vehicles, scuttled tanks and dead horses, surrendered in droves.

The Allies estimated that 50,000 prisoners had been taken. 10,000 German corpses were found on the battlefield. Between 20,000 and 40,000 Germans had, therefore, managed to escape... but only towards another trial, that of the Seine.

ON THE ROAD TO FALAISE

Despite two massive attacks along the Caen – Falaise road on 9 August 1944, the Canadians and Poles were blocked fifteen kilometres from their objective. The British 53rd Division, initially in action in the Odon valley, crossed the Orne and was sent to the Laize valley on the flank of the German defences. On 12 August at Bois-Halbout, these Welshmen came up against the 271. Infanterie-Division. The attempt to outflank them came to nothing

and on the 14th, the attack was resumed on the main axis, supported by 800 heavy bombers. The Germans were battered and on 16 August, the Canadians infiltrated Falaise by the north-west.

Bearing the name of the commander of the 271. Infanterie-Division, this sign was found in 1994 at Cesny-Bois-Halbout (Calvados), indicating a fording point over the Orne or one of its tributaries.

ROYAL WELCH FUSILIERS

On 16 August, the order was issued for a retreat beyond the river Dives, but the German high command demanded that Falaise be solidly held and that a powerful attack widen the exit in the Argentan sector. On the ground, Falaise was already lost and the

surrounded troops were no longer capable of launching an offensive. On 17 August, the British 53rd Division was once more facing the 271. Infanterie-Division west of Falaise. The grenadiers held for two days before the Welsh created a six kilometre breakthrough as far as Nécy.

This helmet belonged to a soldier of the Royal Welch Fusiliers of the 53rd (Welsh) Infantry Division. This pre-war pattern, found in this configuration in Normandy, highlights the service of this regular army unit since 1939.

LECLERC'S BOYS

On the afternoon of 13 August, a patrol of the French 2e division blindée (2nd French Armoured Division) briefly entered into Argentan. Landed on 1 August at Utah Beach, 'Leclerc's boys' were cheered throughout Normandy and joined the US XV Corps at Alençon on 9 August. Having just chased the 9. Panzer-Division from the Ecouves forest, they would have to, along with the 90th US Infantry Division, hold the lower jaw of the pincer against the Germans holding on at Argentan.

This water bottle belonged to a veteran of the 2e division blindée. Their equipment, from tanks to mess tins, was American-made. A bag strap has been added so that the canteen can be slung in the French way.

PANZERGRUPPE EBERBACH

Upon arriving in the Argentan sector, the Germans withdrawing from Mortain were forced to go onto the defensive. The plans for a massive attack by Panzergruppe Eberbach towards Alençon or Mêle-sur-Sarthe were abandoned on 13 August. Instead of a breakthrough shattering the American front, this force carried out local attacks in order to keep open the breach from Argentan to Falaise and allowing two German armies to flee. In the afternoon of 16 August, elements of the 116. Panzer-Division and 2. SS-Panzer-Division attacked the 90th US Infantry Division at Bourg-Saint-Léonard. The fighting continued until the evening of the following day.

This group, comprising of a belt, two ammunition pouches and an other ranks' Waffen-SS cap, was found in an attic at Silly-en-Gouffern, between Argentan and Bourg-Saint-Léonard at the end of the 1980s.

CANADIAN SCOTTISH

Although the American staffs were at the origin of the 'small encirclement' at Falaise on 15 August, they estimated that the bulk of the German forces had already escaped. So half of XV Corps left towards the Seine for a wide outflanking manoeuvre. In reality, the German armies had only begun pulling back during the night of the 16th. Calling for coordinated attacks towards Trun and Chambois on 17 August, Montgomery committed two armoured divisions to close the pocket. The following day, Trun was taken, and reconnaissance units reached Saint-Lambert-sur-Dives (Canadians) and Chambois (Polish). On 19 August, the Canadian 3rd Division was fighting on the east bank of the Dives whilst two armoured regiments and three Polish battalions captured the northern part of Hill 262 at Montormel. On the same evening, more Poles were at Chambois and linked up with the 90th US Infantry Division.

This British Mark III helmet belonged to a soldier of the 1st Canadian Scottish, 3rd Canadian Infantry Division. It was found in 2013 at Barou-en-Auge near Trun.

ESCAPE WITH MEINDL

On 19 August, General Meindl, commander of the 2nd paratrooper corps, saw that the "lid was on the cauldron". He had to force a way through beneath Trun and take Montormel in order to extract as many troops as possible from the Falaise pocket. After crossing the Dives, the paratroopers were stopped at Coudehard by artillery fire on the morning of 20 August. Helped by tank attacks against the Poles, Meindl held the road from Coudehard to Champosoult in the afternoon. The German columns escaped.

The writing in his Soldbuch (pay book) is unambiguous. This administrative officer of the II. Fallschirmjäger-Korps had taken part in the fighting to force a way out of the Falaise-Argentan pocket during the night of 19 to 20 August 1944.

HORSES DIE TOO

On 20 August, the 353. Infanterie-Division, which had taken three hours to get out of Tournai-sur-Dives through destroyed vehicles, abandoned tanks and dead horses, crossed the Moissy ford, leaving behind its vehicles and guns. The XLVII. Panzer-Korps opened a route via Saint-Lambert-sur-Dives as far as Coudehard despite the incredible jams on the roads. Slowed down by the latter, other units, under constant artillery fire, had to fight their own way out of the Corridor of Death.

This axle grease tin from a German carriage is a reminder that the infantry division's transportation was still mainly horse-drawn. It is estimated that almost 10,000 horses were killed and that 2,000 carriages were abandoned in the Falaise Pocket.[1]

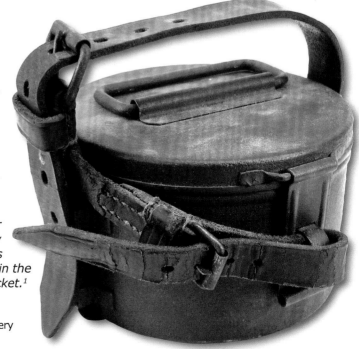

---

1. As a comparison, in the Pocket there were 200 tanks, 1,000 artillery pieces and 5,000 other abandoned vehicles.

CHAMBOIS AND THE SLEDGEHAMMER

On 20 August, 1,500 Poles and 80 tanks were surrounded at Montormel. They had to face tank attacks from outside the pocket, as well as determined assaults from grenadiers and parachutists from within. They could no longer stem the flow of Germans around Hill 262. In Chambois, the 10th Dragoons and the 24th Lancers (1st Polish Armoured Division), supported by the Americans, repulsed attack after attack. Because of its shape, but above all because of the fighting which took place there, Hill 262 became known in Polish as the "Maczuga" (sledgehammer). The division lost 330 killed, more than a thousand wounded and 120 missing. [1]

This battledress blouse belonging to a cavalry corporal of the 24th Lancers is that of the combat dress. A fire on board the tank, the nightmare of all tank crews, has left the imprint of the NCO's webbing equipment.

1. From *L'épopée de la 1ʳᵉ Division Blindée Polonaise*, by Stéphane Brière and Michel Pépin (Association nationale des anciens combattants et du souvenir de la 1ʳᵉ DB polonaise) – Ysec Editions, 2004.

SAINT-LAMBERT-SUR-DIVES

On 20 August, the LXXXIV. and LXXIV. Armee-Korps, covering the rear of the German breakout, attempted to escape the trap. These remains of infantry divisions fought for the most part at Saint-Lambert-sur-Dives and the Moissy ford. At Saint-Lambert, a little under 200 men and twenty Canadian tanks of the South Alberta Regiment, commanded by Major Currie[1], were tasked with blocking this fleeing mass at the river Dives.

This tank crew helmet was found in a farm at Ecorchés, north-east of Trun in the 1990s. The black and yellow flash identifies the South Alberta Regiment, the reconnaissance unit of the Canadian 4th Armoured Division.

1. Major Dave Currie, commanding C Squadron of the South Alberta Regiment, was decorated with the Victoria Cross for his actions at Saint-Lambert-sur-Dives.

THE POCKET IS CLOSED

On 21 August, Canadian reinforcements reached the Poles at Montormel and relieved Major Currie. Saint-Lambert-sur-Dives was at last secured and only a few groups of Germans managed to slip away. The fighting in the Falaise Pocket was coming to a close, but it was not exactly a Normandy version of Stalingrad. Most of the headquarters staffs had managed to flee. Despite having lost most of their strength, these units would rise again and fight in the Ardennes.

These badges and decorations are those of a German Panzer officer killed in the Tournai-sur-Dives sector. From left to right: Tank combat badge, Iron Cross 1st Class, wound badge and the German Cross in Gold, awarded for "acts of exceptional or repeated bravery, or for merit linked to repeated and exceptional command".

GENERAL BADINSKI

On 19 August 1944, General Curt Badinski was preparing to extract his 276. Infanterie-Division from the Falaise Pocket. Out of contact, he had to wait until three in the morning during the night of 19-20 August before receiving his orders from the LXXIV. Armee-Korps. He was to gather his men together in the Vorché sector on the Trun – Occagnes road, then escape south of Trun from 08.30 hrs onwards. Badinski got going, but very soon realised that this undertaking, carried out in daylight and under the threat of artillery and aircraft, was doomed to fail. He countermanded the move, hoping to start again towards the east after dark. Before the end of the day, his HQ on the edge of the Gouffern forest was surrounded by tanks of the British 11th Armoured Division and Badinski, his staff and the bulk of his men were captured.

This gas mask tin belonged to General Badinski. It was found in a junk shop near Flers in the 1990s. The base bears the name (preceded by the rank) of the general and the top bears traces of a white number 1.

Retreat and pursuit

Since breaking out at Avranches, Patton had fought his own war like a cavalry charge, to such an extent that he had to keep a careful eye on gasoline and rations.

With Montgomery and Bradley closing the Falaise Pocket, on 20 August, Patton's armour had reached Chartres and Orléans. An infantry division had crossed the Seine at Mantes. Towards the mouth of the Seine, the great encirclement of the Germans in Normandy had begun, whereas south of Paris, four bridgeheads had been conquered between Melun and Troyes.

In Paris, von Choltitz had received the order to defend the city like a fortress. Meanwhile, the Vichy government officials were abandoning police stations, town halls and ministries. The Resistance took over these buildings but, fearing a German backlash, they called upon the Swedish consul to negotiate a truce that would allow them to wait for the Allied armies. Von Choltitz maintained order in Paris with 5,000 men and organised its exterior defence with 20,000 others.

For the Allies, Paris was of lesser strategic use than the Seine, but for Général De Gaulle, the head of the provisional government, its liberation was at the top of the agenda.

Leclerc and his armoured division were given the order to drive hard and enter Paris. However, the going was not as easy as hoped for and a detachment of troops only reached the city hall on the 24th around midnight. The surrender was signed on the 25th. Paris had not burned and – symbolically – Hitler had lost France.

With the Seine crossed, the situation called for pursuit. However, only the port of Cherbourg was in use and the Allies were still lacking an indispensable logistical base.

On 25 August, the Americans launched their attack on Brest and on 2 September, the British attacked Le Havre. But, the bombing and the siege of these two fortresses had wrought great damage to their infrastructure.

The British and Canadian armies were now launched into northern France and Belgium, as far as the area around Antwerp. By mid-September, the American armies of Normandy and Provence had linked-up. However, the pursuit came to an end, the Germans would now be defending their Vaterland.

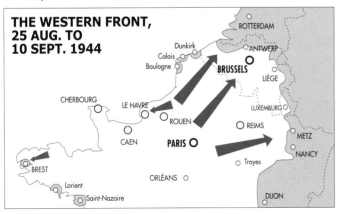

THE WESTERN FRONT, 25 AUG. TO 10 SEPT. 1944

ROTTERDAM
Dunkirk
Calais
Boulogne
ANTWERP
BRUSSELS
LIÈGE
CHERBOURG
LE HAVRE
LUXEMBURG
ROUEN
CAEN
REIMS
PARIS
METZ
NANCY
Troyes
ORLÉANS
BREST
Lorient
Saint-Nazaire
DIJON

FIRST AT THE RIVER

On 20 August, Patton announced that he held a bridgehead over the Seine. The previous day, crossing a dam north of Rolleboise, an officer and two men of the 79th US Infantry Division were the first Americans to reach the right bank. Starting at Le Mêle-sur-Sarthe, by 15 August they were at Nogent-le-Roi when the order came to take Mantes-Gassicourt[1] and block areas where the Germans pouring back from Normandy could pass. Capturing Mantes on the 19th and working non-stop,

the 79th took across a whole battalion to the right bank on the morning of 20 August. The engineers laid down a bridge at Rosny-sur-Seine in order to get the tanks across.

This American pistol belt was found at Bréval, fifteen kilometres to the west of Mantes-la-Jolie. It bears shell splinter damage.

―――――

1. Mantes-la-Jolie was, prior to 1953, known as Mantes-Gassicourt, stemming from the merging of the towns of Mantes-sur-Seine and Gassicourt.

LA FERRIÈRE SUR RISLE

Amongst the 400 aircraft which dropped their bombs into the Risle valley on 17 August were sixty twin-engine B26 Marauders of the 387th Bombardment Group. The report for mission No 219 mentions objectives such as Pont-Audemer, Montfort-sur-Risle, Brionne, Nassandres, Beaumontel, Beaumont-le-Roger and La Ferrière-sur-Risle. The previous day, mission No 217 had targeted Pont-Audemer, Thibouville, Brionne and Nassandres. Here, the bombers tried to destroy all of the bridges along a fifty-kilometre stretch of the river and block the German retreat towards Rouen and the Seine.

These photos, showing the destruction caused by the air raid, have been carefully framed and kept in memory of 17 August 1944, when 23 civilians were killed by bombs at La Ferrières-sur-Risle.

THE GREAT ENCIRCLEMENT

With the bridgehead established at Mantes-Gassicourt, the task now was to prevent a German force, pushed from Falaise by the British and Canadians and estimated at 75,000 men and 250 tanks, from reaching the Seine. The 2nd US Armored Division reached the suburbs of Elbeuf on 24 August. Between the Eure and Seine rivers, the 5th US Armored Division came up against a combat group protecting the crossing points from Vernon to Les

Andelys. The Germans held on for five days, assisted by the fog and rain, and making the most of the small valleys and woods to conceal themselves. The next day, in the morning of 25 August, the Americans relinquished the sector to the British who launched an attack on Vernon in the evening of the same day.

This German assault rifle (Sturmgewehr or MP43/44), was found outside Louviers, on the road to Elbeuf.

OPERATION 'PADDLE'

From 16 August onwards, Operation 'Paddle' involved the British parachutists and commandos who had held the line for two months in the Orne bridgehead. They were reinforced by the Belgian Brigade Piron and the Dutch Brigade 'Princesse Irene' and associated with three British divisions, one of which was armoured. They would pursue the Germans during the course of their successive withdrawals to the rivers Dives, Touques, and Risle and as far as the banks of the Seine. On 23 August, elements of the 6th Airborne Division marched towards Pont-Audemer, which was liberated on the 26th.

This Fairbairn Sykes dagger was a weapon issued to British commandos and parachutists; it was found at Calleville, near Pont-Audemer.

DEFENDING GROSS PARIS

Although the Germans did not have the means nor the intention to fight in the streets of the French capital, they had, on the other hand, maintained strong defensive positions on the entry roads via the west and south-west. As brief and limited as it was, a battle for Paris had preceded the glorious entry of Général Leclerc's 2e DB. Proof of the violence of this fighting, notably at Toussus-le-Noble, Massy and Fresnes can be found in the fact that by the evening of 24 August, the division had lost almost 300 men, forty tanks and a hundred vehicles.

This Luftwaffe (air force) helmet was found in Paris. The German air force was particularly well represented on the outer defensive ring, as many 88 mm anti-aircraft guns had been set up to as a defence against the tanks.

VON CHOLTITZ SURRENDERS

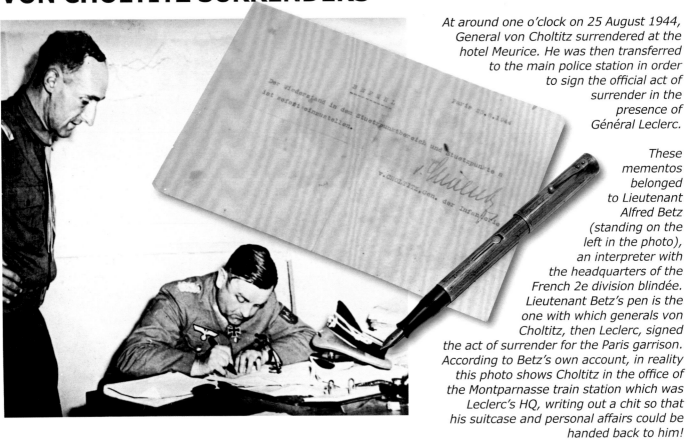

At around one o'clock on 25 August 1944, General von Choltitz surrendered at the hotel Meurice. He was then transferred to the main police station in order to sign the official act of surrender in the presence of Général Leclerc.

These mementos belonged to Lieutenant Alfred Betz (standing on the left in the photo), an interpreter with the headquarters of the French 2e division blindée. Lieutenant Betz's pen is the one with which generals von Choltitz, then Leclerc, signed the act of surrender for the Paris garrison. According to Betz's own account, in reality this photo shows Choltitz in the office of the Montparnasse train station which was Leclerc's HQ, writing out a chit so that his suitcase and personal affairs could be handed back to him!

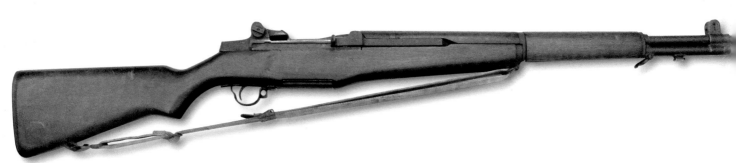

THE FIRST BATTLE FOR BREST

Like Cherbourg, Brest was to become a port of entry for the men and materiel which would launch the final assault on the Reich. Thus, on 25 August, the first battle for Brest began. Low on artillery ammunition – and with the supporting air raids having had little effect on the fortifications – three American infantry divisions were forced to deal with the strongpoints one by one. On 27 August, the 175th Infantry Regiment took Plouzané, but it would take another week before Hill 103 was captured.

This semi-automatic M-1 rifle belonged to Private Joe Barnes (E Company, 175th Infantry Regiment, 29th US Infantry Division) killed on 27 August in the Plouzané cemetery.

CROSSING THE SEINE

All of the Germans west of the Seine received the order to withdraw during the night of 26 August. By the 29th, almost all of the troops and three-quarters of the tanks had crossed the river. Due to this surprising achievement, the Allied staffs ordered an inquest to be held, which revealed that 240,000 men, 30,000 vehicles and 135 tanks had managed to cross the river despite the fact that practically all of the bridges had been destroyed.

The Germans had managed to get troops and equipment across at night at more than sixty different points. The main sites were a pontoon bridge at Poses, near Elbeuf and the railway bridge at Rouen. But they had also largely used the ferries at Duclair, Caudebec or Villequier, and when this was not the case had just simply made rafts out of barn doors and empty fuel barrels.

These two Germans helmets were left behind on the left bank of the Seine and were found together in a house in Orival just to the north of Elbeuf.

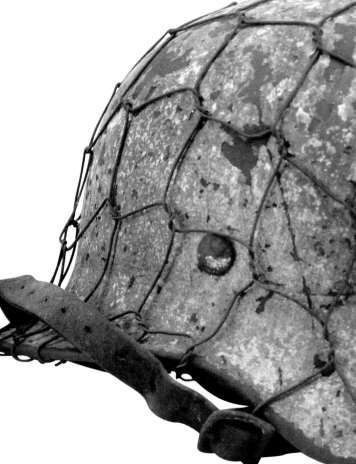

GEN. RAMCKE'S LAST FIGHT

After two weeks of violent combat on the hills overlooking Brest, the battle changed. On 7 September, the requests made by General Middleton[1] seemed to be getting somewhere. He would soon have more artillery ammunition than he really needed. The next day, his three divisions advanced behind a powerful artillery barrage. On the 9th, two of them were in Brest and on the 12th, the 29th was in front of the Keranroux and Montbarey forts. On 13 September, Ramcke refused to surrender and the siege of the forts began.

Keranroux fell, but it took an air raid and the support of British flamethrowing tanks to subdue Montbarey (16 September) and force open the Recouvrance defences. On the 17th, the forts on the west coast were neutralised. On the 18th, with the troops in the town surrendering, General Ramcke gave himself up on the Crozon peninsula, in a coastal artillery battery at the Pointe des Capucins.

This walking stick with sculpted dog's head belonged to General der Fallschirmtruppe Hermann-Bernard Ramcke and had been presented to him by the men of his brigade in North Africa, 1942.

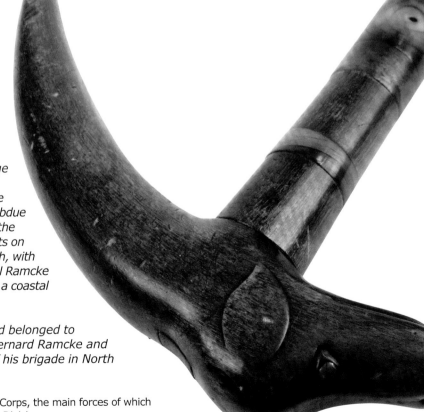

---

1. General Middleton commanded the VIIIth US Corps, the main forces of which comprised of the 2nd, 8th, and 29th US Infantry Divisions.

THE RUINS OF LE HAVRE

On 12 September, guided by the FFI, British tanks were driving through Le Havre. At 11.30 hrs, the Germans capitulated.
Since 5 June, more than 2,300 of Le Havre's citizens had been killed or posted as missing and the town was 80%[1] destroyed. Like the Americans at Brest, the British had had to take a port whilst the bulk of the troops chased the Germans as far as Belgium. With two infantry divisions in front of the fortress, that the Germans had sworn to defend to the last man, the British prepared an attack mainly with heavy bombers. But 60,000 civilians still had not been evacuated...

This cyclist's jacket bearing the French national colours on the breast as well as an armband on the left sleeve was worn by a member of the Le Havre Resistance.

―――――
1. 98% of the village of Fontaine-la-Mallet, bombed on 9 and 10 September 1944 was damaged.

THE END OF THE PURSUIT

On the other bank of the Seine, the German troops that had withdrawn from Normandy did not manage to re-establish a line of defence. The Allies kept the pressure up and set the Ruhr as the new objective. By 3 September they were in Brussels and in Antwerp the following day. However, the Germans had dug in a new line beyond the Scheldt, and the pursuit was over.

This woman's beret, embroidered with flags, illustrates the happy moments when Allied troops were held up by the acclamations of the liberated populations... more than by the enemy, busy falling back to the Siegfried Line.

AFTER THE BATTLE

As the dust settled in Normandy, the sound of gunfire echoed through the foothills of the Vosges.

The Germans, who had committed less than a million men in Normandy, had lost almost 450,000, including 200,000 prisoners. Of the two million Allied soldiers who had landed by 30 August 1944, more than 250,000 had been killed or wounded. It is estimated that 35 German divisions had been wiped-out and 1,500 tanks, 2,000 artillery guns and 20,000 vehicles destroyed.

But more than these statistics, the rapidity with which the Allies had crossed France after Normandy highlights the decisive nature of this battle. It brought with it the hope of a rapid end to the war. Borne by this momentum, young Norman men joined up as Allied convoys passed by.

The Germans, however, would hold on. The Allies, by attempting to go around the Westwall defences via Holland, suffered a failure at Arnhem. They then had to endure a winter of snow and fire between the Vosges and the Alsace plain, as well as being counter-attacked in the Ardennes before reaching the Rhine.

Seen from Normandy, these faraway regions appeared closer as the motor convoys of the Red Ball Express, delivering 12,000 tonnes of supplies on a daily basis, seemed to reduce the distances.

But the war and all its sorrows was not totally gone. Before long, the field hospitals filled up once again with the wounded brought back from these distant fronts. The landings had also caused many French civilian casualties: in the five departments of the Manche, Calvados, Orne, Eure and Seine-Inferieure, the number of dead civilians reached 20,000, half the number of the Americans killed in action and more than those of the British and Canadian combined.

Whilst waiting to learn of the fate of their own men in captivity in Germany, the French lived alongside German POWs. The latter worked with young French civilians in the thankless task of burying the dead and clearing the region of ammunition and mines. And even though they were unaware of the fact that even more ferocious battles had taken place in the East, the photo of a Soviet soldier raising the flag on top of the Reichstag in Berlin brought a sense of relief.

On 8 May 1945, the war was at last over and the French prisoners of war could return home.

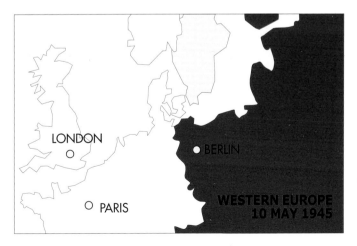

LONDON
○

● BERLIN

○ PARIS

**WESTERN EUROPE
10 MAY 1945**

A SON'S RETURN....

After the battle, the war graves services set up provisional cemeteries. These units, often helped by German prisoners and French civilians, buried the dead of both sides. Thus, at Orglandes, the remains of more than 6,000 Germans were interred by the American Graves Registration Service.

This pay book belonged to a German artilleryman of the 353. Infanterie-Division, killed on 2 July 1944 (transferred from Brittany, the division defended La Haye du Puits) and buried on the 6th at Orglandes. The award certificate for the Iron Cross Second Class, received on the Eastern Front in 1942, illustrates the fate of this unit which was practically wiped-out in Russia in November 1943 and whose survivors were incorporated into the 353. The letter from the International Committee of the Red Cross and the certificate of the German bureau for information of families of soldiers fallen in action with the former Wehrmacht [1] were mailed to the family in 1946 and 1947 in confirmation of his death and place of burial. After the war, the remains were brought home and interred in the military section of his home town cemetery, in Rhineland Palatinate, less than twenty kilometres from the French border.

<hr>

1. 'Deutsche Dienststelle für die Benachrichtigung der nächsten Angehörigen von Gefallenen der ehemaligen deutschen Wehrmacht,' controlled by the American military government of occupied Germany.

AN AMERICAN
IN BRITTANY

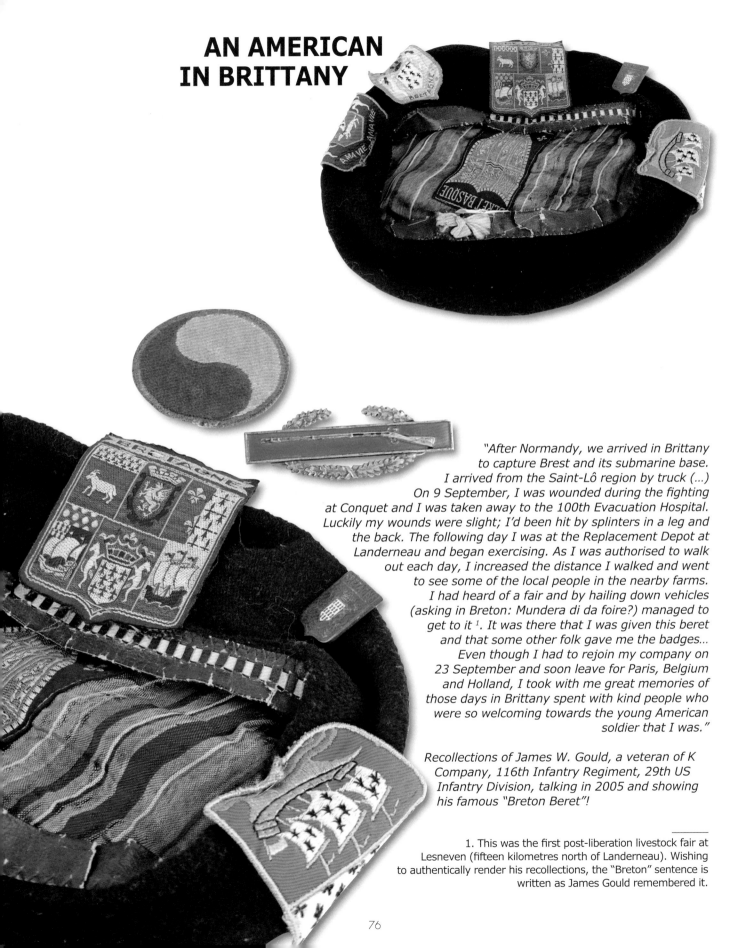

"After Normandy, we arrived in Brittany to capture Brest and its submarine base. I arrived from the Saint-Lô region by truck (…) On 9 September, I was wounded during the fighting at Conquet and I was taken away to the 100th Evacuation Hospital. Luckily my wounds were slight; I'd been hit by splinters in a leg and the back. The following day I was at the Replacement Depot at Landerneau and began exercising. As I was authorised to walk out each day, I increased the distance I walked and went to see some of the local people in the nearby farms. I had heard of a fair and by hailing down vehicles (asking in Breton: Mundera di da foire?) managed to get to it [1]. It was there that I was given this beret and that some other folk gave me the badges… Even though I had to rejoin my company on 23 September and soon leave for Paris, Belgium and Holland, I took with me great memories of those days in Brittany spent with kind people who were so welcoming towards the young American soldier that I was."

Recollections of James W. Gould, a veteran of K Company, 116th Infantry Regiment, 29th US Infantry Division, talking in 2005 and showing his famous "Breton Beret"!

1. This was the first post-liberation livestock fair at Lesneven (fifteen kilometres north of Landerneau). Wishing to authentically render his recollections, the "Breton" sentence is written as James Gould remembered it.

SOUVENIRS OF AUSTRIA

Before their units were disbanded, many Resistance fighters joined the new regiments of the French army. On 17 August, the 1er régiment automobile 'Bretagne' was formed. Driving from Omaha Beach, the young French volunteers drove American trucks to supply Patton's 3rd US Army. The 'Bretagne' along with four other regiments (Normandie, Anjou, Maine and Paris) next formed the TMAPC[1]. Up to September 1945, they first supplied the liberated populations, and then took back wounded men and prisoners, driving across France, Germany, Austria and Czechoslovakia.

These souvenirs, a 6.35 calibre 1910 model Mauser pistol and an embroidered version of the German Cross in Gold (see page 64), were brought back from Austria by a member of the FFI who had enlisted in the 1er régiment automobile 'Bretagne.'

1. Transports Militaires Automobiles pour les Populations Civiles.

THE SWEET TASTE OF FREEDOM

Although all of the supply problems were far from solved in the immediate post-war period, the Liberation brought great hopes with it. The French children were crazy about the chocolate bars that the GIs so generously handed out, and most of them would forever associate the particular taste of these treats with freedom at last.

Chewing gum and cigarettes are also associated with the first moments of the Liberation, but other products which have become commonplace since also arrived with American rations... This is true of the 'Mars' bar which was sold in France from 1951 onwards, but which had been made in Great Britain and the United States since 1932.

PRISONER OF WAR

At Foucarville (Manche), 15 September 1944, Evacuation Enclosure No 1, a transit camp for prisoners departing via Utah Beach for Great Britain or the United States, became the Continental Central Enclosure No 19, a complex designed to hold 20,000 prisoners. During the course of 1945 it held an average 30,000. It was a fully-fledged town where joiners, carpenters, blacksmiths, mechanics, shoesmiths and

tailors worked. The camp's bakery supplied 20 tonnes of bread per day and meals were distributed thanks to a narrow-gauge train and seven kilometres of rail recovered from the Atlantic Wall. The camp had its own electricity network, several cinemas and theatres, at least two churches and one thousand-bed hospital.

This garment, from a former German POW who had stayed at Foucarville, is a First World War American tunic, altered by one of the camp's tailors. The armband has been sewn directly onto the sleeve and stamped by the American authorities to attest the status of the wearer as a member of the sanitary personnel. 31G is the prefix of the prisoner's number (G for German and 31 for the place of capture, ETO for European Theater of Operations).

THE 'CIGARETTE' CAMPS

Named 'Lucky Strike,' 'Old Gold,' 'Twenty Grand,' 'Philip Morris,' 'Herbert Tareyton' and 'Pall Mall,' these transit camps, managed by the 89th US Infantry Division and built throughout the Pays de Caux region, housed the GIs awaiting to return home via Le Havre. Between May 1945 and August 1946, a little over 3.5 million soldiers passed through them. And a little later came through approximately 6,000 French 'GI brides.' In January 1946, the first of them left in a special convoy for the New World.

This American helmet liner bearing the insignia of the 89th US Infantry Division was found at Sainte-Marguerite-sur-Duclair, near Camp 'Twenty Grand.'

AS LONG AS IT SAVES...

The French, forced to be resourceful during the German occupation, kept the habit after the Liberation. In Normandy, by foraging around on the battlefield, all sorts of useful objects were salvaged, whatever their actual use would be. The euphoria of freedom soon gave way to the hard reality of having to rebuild, and anything that could be used was.

This oxygen bottle "found on the battlefield in August 1944," despite being German, came in handy after the war. As the period label states, "It brought back to life" two people who had suffocated in a mine shaft in 1947 and "also helped to cure children stricken with pneumonia".

THE MOST HAZARDOUS JOB

In October 1944, after eight days' training at the British Royal Engineers Mines School at Bayeux, the French volunteers of the '3e bataillon du génie' were put to work. By October 1945, these young sappers from Normandy, Mayenne and Paris had cleared 60,000 mines. They then trained civilians of the French ministries of rural utilities and reconstruction. After the end of the war, German prisoners of war joined these teams and ended up making 90% of their strength. Most of the mine-clearing was completed by the end of 1947. In France, 13 million mines and 17 million projectiles had been removed and destroyed at the cost of 2,500 killed and 5,000 wounded. Within the ranks of the 3e bataillon de génie, 18 volunteer bomb disposal sappers were killed and 25 wounded.

This jumping mine, wooden antipersonnel mine, three-headed pressure/pull fuse, and badge are the souvenirs of caporal-chef Gilbert Paquet, from the town of Sées. He volunteered on 15 September 1944 and was attached at the end of the month to the 3e bataillon de génie.

George Patton (Pat) Waters

The author of the foreword, George Patton (Pat) Waters, is the grandson of the famous general, George Smith Patton, Jr. (1885-1945). He is the son of Beatrice (the eldest daughter of General Patton) and General John K. Waters. An officer in the US Navy Reserve from 1965 to 1970, he served on *USS Braine* and carried out a three-year Western Pacific Tour off the coast of Vietnam. Living in South Carolina, he has made the most of his early retirement, sailing and flying. Pat remains very involved in local life and within many organisations. He is the vice-chairman of the board of directors at the Mount Pleasant Roper Hospital. A skilled pilot, he plays an active role with the Charleston County Aviation Authority and Air Safety Foundation.

Finally, amongst other activities and responsibilities, George Patton Waters is a member of the Congressional Medal of Honor Foundation and has also put time into the creation of a National Medal of Honor Museum dedicated to those who have been awarded this decoration.

Régis Giard

The author is a 38-year old from Normandy who has lived in Le Havre since 2004 and whose parental families come from the Manche department between La Haye du Puits and Lessay. He has been interested in the fighting of 1944 in his region since his childhood. Régis Giard (known as 'Reggie' to the veterans and their families), concentrated from the mid-1990s onwards on the 79th US Infantry Division. He has taken part in bringing veterans back to France and has accompanied families of soldiers during their pilgrimages in Normandy. His research included visits on the battlefield, interviews with witnesses of the events and studies in various archives, notably at the East Carolina University, where he worked on the personal papers of the divisional commander in 1944, General Wyche.

In 2008, in collaboration with Frédéric Blais, he wrote 'Helmets of the ETO,' also published by Histoire & Collections. Since then, Régis Giard has regularly authored articles in military history publications.

Since 2012, he has been involved with the 79th Sustainment Support Command (SSC), which upholds the 79th Division's traditions.

Recovered from the battlefield at Montormel-Coudehard, the remains of a British Mk III Sten SMG, a German MP40 SMG, and the stock for a German paratroopers' light machine gun (FG42).

This tin box, saved from a refuse dump at Douvres la Délivrande, contains several British and Canadian cap badges, collected in 1944.

Acknowledgements:
For their help in producing this book, the author wishes to thank:
George Patton Waters, Pierre-François Boselli, Philippe Charbonnier, Major General Megan Tatu, Colonel Kristen Dixon, William « Doc » Long and his family, the relatives of Leslie R. Brantingham, Kenneth J. McDonald's family, Karine and Noël Giard, Frédéric Blais, Tyler Alberts, Jacquelyn Todd, Sue Templeman, Henri Levaufre, Yann Renaud, Emmanuel Doucet, Thierry Monnier, Gaëtan Hamel, Denis Toutain, Jean-Yves Durel, Gilles Orlando, Céline and Pierre-Louis Gosselin, Arnaud Bertaux, Dominic Biello, Laurent Valleroy, Anne-Sophie Goubet-Druon, Didier Lehay, Hubert and Dominique Herbert, David Brunet, Arnaud Dumont, Pascal Hourblin, Stéphane Lepaysant, David Dufour, Benoît Beauquesne, Manuel Lehoussu, Arnaud Dudouit, Stéphane Martinez, Claude Lesouef, Christophe Lambert, Stéphane Jonot, Frédéric Normand, Stéphane Brière, Florian Poté, Bruno Polveri, Patrick Hinchy, Doris Davis, Emilie and Francis Weyl, Jérôme Autret, Yves Tannière, Alexis Boban, Bruno Nion, Erwan Omnes, Yannick Creac'h, Eric Pilon, and Gwenäel Blotin.

The author can be reached through his Facebook page

Captions of cover, etc. pictures:

– Front cover: US Army captain's helmet liner found at Montgardon, near La Haye-du-Puits
– Page 3: clothing issue records book for a German sapper unit present at Arromanches on 6 June 1944, mentioning the loss of 932 soldiers.
– Outside back cover: American grenades painted blue, white and red during the Liberation and found at Marigny.

Photo credits:
US Army via Tyler Alberts (pages 1, 5, 12, 14, 20, 21, 22, 23, 44, 45, 46, 52, 54, 72, 74) - George Patton Waters (pages 5, 82) - Imperial War Museum (page 8) - Bundesarchiv (pages 12, 27, 28, 36, 59, 65, 66) - Big Red One Museum (page 16) – Kieffer family via Eric Le Penven (page 19) – Stéphane Martinez (Page 20) - McDonald family (page 25) – Leslie Cruise via Sue Templeman and Dominic Biello (page 29) – Bibliothèque et Archives Canada (pages 40, 58, 64) - Australian War Museum (page 42) - David Brunet (page 49) - Emilie and Francis Weyl (page 70) - Yannick Creac'h (page 70) – Jérôme Autret (page 80) – 79th Sustainment Support Command (Page 82) - Régis Giard (all other pictures).

Edited by Philippe Charbonnier - Design and layout by Philippe Charbonnier and Nathalie Sanchez for Histoire & Collections
Translated from the French by Lawrence Brown
© Histoire & Collections 2014

Book edited by
HISTOIRE & COLLECTIONS
SA au capital de 182 938, 82 €
5, avenue de la République - F-75541 Paris Cedex 11
Tél: +33 (0) 1 40 21 18 20 - Fax: +33 (0) 1 47 00 51 11
www.histoireetcollections.com

This book has been designed, typed, laid-out and processed by Histoire & Collections on fully integrated computer equipment.

Printed in May 2014 by Calidad Grafica, Spain, European Union.